EQUITY AND COMPASSION IN INCLUSIVE SOCIAL ENGAGEMENT

DR. A. SYLVIA DAISY
DR. N. JOSHUA JAYASEELAN
DR. JANICE SHIJI

Made with ❤on the Notion Press Platform

www.notionpress.com

Dedication

This book is dedicated to all those who work towards creating an Inclusive Society, especially to all the participants and organisers of the Study Conference titled "Equity and Compassion in Inclusive Social Engagement" organised on 29th November, 2024 m, Madras Christian College, East Tambaram, Chennai, Tamil Nadu, India.

Department of Social Work (SFS),

Madras Christian College, Chennai, Tamil Nadu, India

Contents

Dedication

Contents

Foreword

Preface

Acknowledgement

Prologue

1. Street Art and Social Inclusion in Tamil Nadu

Dr. V. Chitra

2. Ashoka and Inclusiveness

Ms. Aleena Elizabeth

3. Inclusiveness through the Art Forms in India

Ms. Gayathri. K

4. Dialogue on Gender, Social Justice and Inclusiveness: A Field Perspective on Policies for Social Inclusion and Equity

Dr. Karunya Devi. N

5. Promoting Social Inclusion through Employment: Assessing the Socio-Economic Impact of MGNREGA in Rural Communities of Chengalpattu

Ms. Tharani. T, Jacob Steyns & Dr. S. Sudharsan

6. A Study on the Social Challenges Faced by the Queer Community in Chennai

Ms. Maria Jayanthi Jerome & Ms. Nisha

7. Silent Suffering: Leadership neglect and the Caste chains of Sanitation Workers in India

Mr. J. P. Francis Dhivakar

8.புறந்தள்ளலைப் புறந்தள்ளும் புறநானூற்றுப் பாடல்கள்

முனைவர் த. செபுலோன் பிரபு துரை

9. A Study on the Challenges faced by Transgenders

Ms. Minulin Beaulah. A, Ms. Raghu Nandhini.K, Mr. Samuel Surendran. J & Dr. Baily Vincent

10. Religio-philosophical foundation as a coping mechanism for Exile: A case study of Tibetan Refugees

Ms. Shilpa Joseph & Ms. G. K. Rhiya Jency

11. கோத்தகிரி பழங்குடி மக்களின் எண்ணம் எழுத்தாதல்

முனைவர் சி. முத்துகந்தன்

12. A Study on Emotional Well-being of the Elderly Women

Ms. Sharon Mary Rajesh, Ms. Hafiza Abdul Khader & Dr. A. Sylvia Daisy

13. A Study on Parenting Style of Single Parents

Mr. Ajay Kumar. R & Mr. Mohan Raj. R

14. A Study on the Impact of Madras Christian College Family Life Institute on Health and Socio-Economic Condition of its Beneficiaries

Jessica Jasmine.R, Jenita Mary. F & Dr. A. Sylvia Daisy

15. Assessing the Efficacy of Assistive Technologies in Improving Communication Skills for People with Multiple Disabilities

Ms. Swetha Anand & Mr. J. P. Francis Dhivakar

16. A Study on the Impact of Climate Change and Marginalization Experienced by Women

Ms. M. V. Akshaya & Dr. Baily Vincent

17. A Study on Substance use and its Influence on Career Development of Youth in Perumbakkam, Chennai

Ms. Trisha Rebecca Leslie & Mr. J. P. Francis Dhivakar

18. The Legacy of Comfort Women and the Path Towards Reconciliation of Historical Injustice

Ms. Caroline Veronica. V

19. A Study on Awareness and Perception of HIV/AIDS among College Students

Ms. A. Arockya Vianny Sweatha & Mr.J.P. Francis Dhivakar

Foreword

The pursuit of an equitable society, one that champions inclusion and compassion, has long been central to India's social fabric. As a nation defined by its diversity—linguistic, cultural, and religious, it is imperative to reflect on how we engage with minorities in ways that affirm dignity, foster equity, and uphold social justice.

Equity and Compassion in Inclusive Social Engagement provides a timely and profound exploration of these themes, addressing the often-neglected intricacies of social inclusion.

In India, minority communities have historically faced significant challenges, ranging from systemic discrimination to marginalization in public life. Despite constitutional safeguards and progressive policies, these communities frequently find themselves excluded from economic opportunities, social privileges, and cultural recognition. This book thoughtfully examines these realities, offering insights into how inclusive social practices, underpinned by compassion, can bridge the gap between legal provisions and lived experiences.

What sets this work apart is its interdisciplinary lens, and distinguished perspectives of various writers- weaving together history, sociology, and lived narratives to underscore the need for empathy-driven policies and grassroots engagement. It reminds us that equity is not just about removing barriers but also about fostering a sense of belonging and shared responsibility.

This is particularly relevant in the Indian context, where social harmony depends on understanding and celebrating pluralism. By addressing the experiences of vulnerable groups—including women, children, single parents, the Irular community, religious minorities, and gender minorities—the book illuminates the urgent need for a collective commitment to justice and compassion in our policies and interactions.

As readers journey through its pages, they are invited to question entrenched biases, embrace inclusion as a core value, and contribute to building a society where every individual, irrespective of their background, has an equal opportunity to thrive.

I am confident that this book, "Equity and Compassion in Inclusive Social Engagement" will serve as a valuable resource for scholars, policymakers, activists, and anyone committed to creating a more just and compassionate world. It is both a call to action and a testament to the transformative power of empathy in shaping inclusive futures.

Dr. Janice Shiji,
Head of the Department- In-Charge,
Department of Social Work (SFS),
Madras Christian College, Chennai

Preface

The book "Equity and Compassion in Inclusive Social Engagement" is an outcome of the Study Conference, organised on 29 November 2024 by the Department of SocialWork, Self Financed Stream, Madras Christian College. The Conference was inaugurated by Fr. E. Sandiyagu, Advocate, High Court of Madras and there were research paper presentations from different disciplines of Humanities such as History, International Studies, Tamil and Social Work on the sub-themes of the Conference, Building Inclusivity, Revitalising Marginalized Communities, Building Alliance through Solidarity and Interfaith Collaboration. The papers presented by the academicians, practitioners and research scholars have been compiled together in this edited book. I hope the readers will enjoy reading these research papers, understand the different perspectives of the authors and contribute towards building an Inclusive Society.

Dr. A. Sylvia Daisy,
Convener, Study Conference,
Associate Professor,
Department of Social Work (SFS),
Madras Christian College, Chennai

Acknowledgement

I express my gratitude to God Almighty for His mercy and grace in organizing the Study Conference and bringing out this book "Equity and Compassion in Inclusive Social Engagement" as an outcome of the Study Conference.

Sincere thanks to Dr. P. Wilson, Principal and Secretary, Madras Christian College, Mr. Cyrus Kallupurackal, Bursar, MCC, Mr. R. Sridhar, Vice-Principal, Administration, MCC, Dr. J. Jannet Vannila, Vice-Principal, Self-Financed Stream, MCC, Dr. K. Ashok and the Program Committee members of Madras Christian College for their precious guidance in organising the Study Conference. Special thanks to Dr. Tabitha, Dean of Research and Development, Madras Christian College, for training our student volunteers in publication work and facilitating this book release through Notion Press.

Heartfelt gratitude to Mr. Andrew Sesuraj. M, President of Professional Social Workers' Association Chennai, and all the members of PSWA for the partnership and networking support in the conduct of the Study Conference. Special thanks to Fr. E. Sandiyagu, Advocate, High Court of Madras and Mr. Cyril Alexander, Vice President, India Network of Professional Social Workers Association being the Chief Guest for the Inaugural and Valedictory Sessions of the Study Conference. Very Special thanks to the Main Representative, Commonwealth Organisation for Social Work, Dr. David N Jones, for addressing the participants on Young Carers and the Charter for Young Carers. Thanks to the moderators of the Plenary Session Dr. K.S. Ramesh, Director, Tata Institute of Social Sciences, Banyan Academy of Leadership and Management, Dr. Tony Kenneth Bharath, University of Madras, Mr. Anthony Rooban, Satya Nilayam, Dr. Yesu Anthony, Director, Family Commission, Diocese of Chengalpattu, and to my colleagues Associate Professor, Dr.V. Chitra, Department of History, Dr. S. Kalyani, Assistant Professor and Dr. Meera Rajeev Kumar, Assistant Professor, Department of Public Administration, Madras Christian College for their contributions and guidance.

I extend my gratitude to Dr. Janice Shiji, Head-In-Charge, Dr. Joshua Jayaseelan, Assistant Professor, to all my colleagues and the student volunteers Ms. Shiloh, Ms. Shirley, Ms. Jessica, Mr. Rohan, and Mr. Samuel Surendran, Department of Social Work, Self-Financed Stream, Madras Christian College for their support in this Book project. Special appreciation to Ms. Shiloh III BSW for her design contributions to the book cover. Last but not the least heartfelt thanks to all the research scholars and teachers for their research papers contributed towards this Book publication.

Dr. A. Sylvia Daisy,
Convener, Study Conference,
Associate Professor,
Department of Social Work (SFS),
Madras Christian College, Chennai

Prologue

The book "Equity and Compassion in Inclusive Social Engagement" is an outcome of the Study Conference, organised on 29 November 2024 by the Department of SocialWork, Self Financed Stream, Madras Christian College. This book contains 19 research papers from different disciplines such as History, International Relations, Social Work and Languages. The authors of the paper have traced the roots of Compassion and Social Inclusion, they have brought out good findings relating to the conditions of the various vulnerable groups such as rural artisans, differently abled, elderly, transgenders, women, people living with HIV/AIDS, marginalized and the tribal groups and most significantly they have made suggestions to various stakeholders for Embracing Diversity and building an Inclusive Society.

Dr. A. Sylvia Daisy,
Convener, Study Conference,
Associate Professor,
Department of Social Work (SFS),
Madras Christian College, Chennai

1. Street Art and Social Inclusion in Tamil Nadu

Dr. V. Chitra
Associate Professor, Department of History,
Madras Christian College, Chennai

Street art, a vibrant and dynamic form of expression has emerged as a powerful tool for social inclusion and cultural revitalization in Tamil Nadu. This form of art transcends mere aesthetics; it serves as a voice for marginalized communities, promotes cultural identity, and fosters social cohesion. By transforming public spaces into canvases for artistic expression, street artists are challenging societal norms, focusing on its ability to give voice to marginalized groups, foster community solidarity This paper examines the multifaceted role of street art in promoting social inclusion in Tamil Nadu.

Street art has evolved beyond its roots in Tamil culture and it became a powerful tool for social expression, activism, and cultural transformation across the globe. As urbanization progressed, these traditional practices began to blend with contemporary artistic expressions, leading to the evolution of street art as we know it today. While the concept of street art as a contemporary art form is relatively new, its roots can be traced back to ancient Tamil culture. Rock art and murals have been integral to Tamil artistic traditions for centuries. These ancient forms of public art served both aesthetic and functional purposes, often depicted as Narratives, historical events, and social customs. In recent years, street art has gained significant popularity in Tamil Nadu; especially in urban centers like Chennai, Coimbatore, and Madurai have become hubs for artistic expression with public spaces.

Street art often reflects the rich cultural heritage of Tamil Nadu. Artists incorporate local themes, symbols, and languages into their work, celebrating regional identity and fostering a sense of belonging among residents. This cultural representation is vital for reinforcing community ties and promoting inclusivity, as it allows individuals to see their stories and experiences reflected in public art. Street art often serves as a celebration of local culture and heritage, reinforcing community identity.

They incorporate traditional symbols, motifs, and narratives that resonate with the local populace, creating a sense of belonging. This art can serve as a powerful medium for addressing social issues such as inequality, discrimination, and environmental degradation. Artists may use their work to raise awareness, provoke thought, and inspire action.

Street art possesses an inherent ability to transcend language barriers and cultural differences. It can evoke emotions, spark conversations, and inspire social change. By visually representing diverse perspectives and experiences, art can challenge stereotypes, promote empathy, and foster a deeper understanding of different cultures. Art can empower individuals to express themselves creatively, enabling them to overcome barriers and share their stories. Street art transforms public spaces into platforms for dialogue, inviting conversations among individuals from various backgrounds. By creating open-air galleries, these artworks encourage social interaction and cultural exchange, helping to bridge divides within multicultural urban environments.

Street art provides a platform for marginalized voices to be heard in urban spaces. The art can be a catalyst for social inclusion by providing a platform for marginalized voices, fostering community engagement, and promoting intercultural dialogue. In Tamil Nadu, artists often create works that reflect the struggles and aspirations of underrepresented groups, thereby asserting their presence in the public realm. By showcasing the work of marginalized artists and art institutions can challenge dominant narratives and promote diverse perspectives. As a form of public art, it allows marginalized communities to assert their presence, challenge dominant narratives, and engage with wider socio-political discourses.

Many street art projects in Tamil Nadu address social issues such as poverty, gender inequality, and discrimination. The themes which empowers the artists by showcasing their stories through art, thereby challenging societal norms and advocating for acceptance. By highlighting the struggles faced by marginalized communities, artists use their work to raise awareness and provoke dialogue. Unlike traditional art confined to galleries, street art occupies urban environments accessible to all. This accessibility challenges notions of ownership over artistic expression and allows marginalized voices to assert their presence in public discourse.

By transforming public spaces into open-air galleries, street art cultivates opportunities for spontaneous interactions among individuals from different walks of life. This democratization of art challenges traditional notions of ownership and access to cultural expression, making it possible for everyone to engage with art outside institutional confines. The presence of street art invites dialogue and fosters mutual respect among community members, enhancing social cohesion.iii

Street art also plays a role in promoting environmental consciousness. Murals that depict nature, wildlife, or environmental degradation serve as visual reminders of ecological issues affecting urban areas. These artworks can inspire community members to engage in sustainability efforts and foster a collective responsibility towards preserving their environment

Street art serves as a catalyst for social change by addressing critical issues such as environmental awareness, gender equality, and human rights. Through powerful imagery and thought-provoking messages, artists can inspire action and dialogue around these topics. For example, campaigns that highlight environmental sustainability through street art encourage community members to engage in discussions about urban living conditions and collective responsibility.

Street art has emerged as an important tool for redefining gender roles and promoting social inclusion for women, particularly those from marginalized communities. Women have long been excluded from positions of power, both in the political and cultural spheres. Gender inequality, particularly in relation to the expectations placed on women in the public and private spheres, has been a central issue for social justice movements in the region.

Women street artists in Tamil Nadu have used their work to challenge patriarchal norms and to create new, empowering representations of women. These works often subvert traditional depictions of femininity, presenting women as strong, autonomous figures who are reclaiming public space. Female artists often use street art to challenge gender stereotypes and advocate for women's rights. Projects associated with events like "International Women's Day" encourage female participation in street art, highlighting issues related to gender bias and empowerment through creative expression

Another key aspect of street art in Tamil Nadu is its role in fostering community-building and collective action. Street art has the potential to bring together diverse groups of people, creating spaces for collaboration, dialogue, and mutual empowerment. Through collaborative art festivals, and community-driven art initiatives, local populations can engage in a process of collective creation that strengthens social ties and promotes inclusion. They involve local residents in the creation of themes and transforming public spaces into community building. This participatory approach fosters a sense of ownership and pride among community members, as they contribute to the artistic representation of their neighborhood.vi Such engagement helps break down social barriers, enabling individuals from diverse backgrounds to connect and collaborate. The participatory nature of street art fosters community engagement by involving local residents in the creation process. Collaborative projects encourage dialogue among diverse groups, breaking down social barriers and promoting inclusivity.

One of the central ways that inclusiveness manifests in contemporary Tamil art is through art's potential for social change. Artists have used their work not just as a reflection of society but as a tool for transforming it. Public art installations, collaborative community projects, and social media platforms have provided new opportunities for marginalized groups to express their concerns, share their stories, and advocate for justice.

Looking ahead, the potential for street art to foster social inclusion in Tamil Nadu remains significant. As urbanization continues and social inequalities persist, street art will likely play an increasingly important role in advocating for marginalized communities and fostering social change. The continued engagement of local communities in street art projects, combined with the growing visibility of street art in the mainstream art world, will help bridge the gap between public and private spaces, making art a more inclusive and accessible form of expression. Nevertheless, the resilience of Tamil street art—its ability to adapt, innovate, and remain relevant in addressing issues of social justice—suggests that it will continue to serve as a powerful form of expression for marginalized communities. Through art, individuals and communities in Tamil Nadu can reclaim public spaces, assert their rights, and build a more inclusive society.

Challenges and Opportunities

Street art has the potential to be a powerful force for social change, it also faces several challenges:

➢ Lack of Recognition and Support: Street artists often lack formal recognition and support from the art establishment.

➢ Vandalism and Destruction: Street art is vulnerable to vandalism and destruction, which can undermine its impact.

To overcome these challenges and maximize the potential of street art, it is essential to:

➢ Promote Art Education: Integrate street art into the school curriculum to encourage creativity and critical thinking.

➢ Support Emerging Artists: Provide opportunities for emerging artists to showcase their work and connect with the art community.

➢ Collaborate with Local Governments and Communities: Work with local authorities and communities to create supportive environments for street art.

To Conclude, Street art in Tamil Nadu has become a significant tool for promoting social inclusion, empowering marginalized communities, and challenging systems of oppression. The art has the power to transform lives and societies. By embracing its potential, we can create a more inclusive, equitable, and compassionate world. By challenging stereotypes, promoting empathy, and empowering marginalized voices, visual art can help to build a more just and equitable future for all.

From addressing caste inequality and gender discrimination to fostering political resistance and community solidarity, street art has proven to be a versatile and powerful medium for social change. As the urban landscape of Tamil Nadu continues to evolve, street art will likely remain a key player in the ongoing struggle for social justice, equality, and inclusivity.

Street art in Tamil Nadu represents more than just visual appeal; it is a dynamic medium for promoting social inclusion and cultural identity. Through various community engagement initiatives, street artists are redefining public spaces while addressing critical social issues faced by marginalized communities. Despite challenges such as legal restrictions and societal perceptions, the continued growth of this movement signifies its importance in shaping an inclusive urban landscape. As Tamil Nadu moves forward, embracing street art as a legitimate form of expression will be essential for fostering dialogue, understanding, and ultimately achieving social cohesion within its diverse communities.

REFERENCES

i Bharadwaj, P. "The Role of Street Art in Social Movements: A Case Study of Tamil Nadu." *South Asian Art Journal*, 2018 14(2), 34-51.

ii Bhan, M., & Gupta, A. *Art and Politics in India: Street Art as Political Activism in Tamil Nadu*. 2016, Chennai: Tamil Nadu State Press.

iii Kavi, A."Reclaiming Public Spaces: The Impact of Street Art in Tamil Nadu." *Urban Culture Review*,2017 6(3), 88-105. iv Ibid.

v Ramaswamy, A. *Gender and Public Art in Tamil Nadu. 2019: Madurai University Press. Madurai, p 48-51 vi Opcit., Kavi A.

vii Madras Art Movement. (2005). *Tamil Contemporary Art: From Tradition to Modernity* 2005. Raman Press, Chennai p 54- 62.

2. Ashoka and Inclusiveness

Ms. Aleena Elizabeth
II MA History, Madras Christian College, Chennai

INTRODUCTION

The Mauryan Empire was the first Pan-Indian empire, encompassing almost all of the subcontinent and even beyond in the northwest. It lasted from c.324-187 BCE. Ashoka's reign spanned from c.273-232 BCE and he was the third ruler in the Mauryan dynasty. Ashoka was the first Indian king who directly spoke to the people through inscriptions, which carried royal orders and proclamations. He is considered one of the great kings in the history of the Indian subcontinent. Ashoka is well known for his policy of Dhamma. Asoka's state policy was driven by Buddhist doctrine, both domestically and internationally. After the destructive Kalinga war, Ashoka converted to Buddhism. Following his ascension to the throne, Ashoka fought just one significant battle, the Kalinga battle (Rock Edict XIII). He claims that 100,000 people were killed during the war. Several lakhs were killed and 150,000 were taken as captives. The figures are overstated due to using 'a hundred thousand' as a cliché in Ashokan inscriptions. The king appears to have been tremendously impacted by the bloodshed in this fight. Therefore, he abandoned the policy of physical occupation. He adopted and started following the policy of Dhamma Vijaya (A country's implementation of the Dhamma policy, rather of territorial control by a war). The policy of Dhamma showcases Ashoka's policies which encompassed inclusiveness.

METHODOLOGY

This study adopts a qualitative research design, focusing on a historical and textual analysis of secondary sources to examine Ashoka's policies and their impact on inclusiveness during his reign. Sources of data are secondary sources such as scholarly books analysing Ashoka's reign and his approach to governance, religion, and social policies. The method of data collection includes a review of existing literature on Ashoka's reign, focusing on themes of inclusiveness, such as religious tolerance, welfare measures, and administrative reforms. The analytical framework includes thematic analysis identifying recurring themes in Ashoka's policies, such as religious pluralism, social justice, and welfare, and contextual analysis which examines the socio-political and religious context of Ashoka's inclusiveness within the framework of Mauryan society.

FINDINGS

12 years after the Abhisheka Ashoka started the practice of having Dhamma inscriptions inscribed in various parts of the empire. To make the principle of Dhamma accessible and understandable to all, Ashoka issued edicts at important points across the empire. During that period, literacy was limited to a small section of society. To ensure the widespread dissemination of his message, Ashoka made extensive arrangements for oral communication by appointing officials such as kumaras, yutas, rajukas, mahamattas, anta-mahamattas, pulisani, and members of the parishad.

The inclusive attitude of Ashoka as a ruler can be seen in many aspects such as his beliefs and policies of religious tolerance, use of multiple languages, non-violence (ahimsa), social welfare policies, protection of the environment, creation of dhamma mahamattas, and dhamma-yatas.

Religious tolerance

Ashoka fostered mutual tolerance and harmony among people from all faiths and religious communities. In Rock Edict VII and Rock Edict XII, he requests for toleration among all sects. A detailed examination of the Rock Edicts reveals Ashoka's desire to foster tolerance and respect for all religious factions, and the role of dhamma mahamatras involved working for both Brahmanas and shramanas.

This edict underscores Ashoka's personal support for religious inclusivity. He stated that all religious sects should be honoured and that their coexistence would contribute to societal unity. He did not engage in mass conversions of people in his empire to the religion he followed or attack other religious institutions like the other emperors in ancient or medieval India had done, which was prevalent during that time.

Ashoka's advocacy of religious tolerance during his reign is particularly important now, especially in an era of increasing diversity in culture, religious pluralism, and interfaith conflict. Ashoka's Dhamma policy, which fostered respect for all religions and ethical living, gives nations valuable lessons about cooperation and understanding. Ashoka's approach emphasizes the need to create inclusive communities in which all ideas are accepted and coexist peacefully. His example can inspire modern governments to develop rules that foster interfaith discussions, defend minority rights, and prevent religious hate speech or discrimination. His dedication to welfare for all, regardless of religious identity, aligns with the current objective of promoting equal opportunity and justice for every citizen. His message is still relevant today, as conflicts driven by religious intolerance continue to endanger global peace.

Use of Multiple Languages

Inscriptions of Ashoka are in the Prakrit language and Brahmi script, as well as the Prakrit language and Kharosthi script. The north-western inscriptions were written in Kharosthi script. Some inscriptions were also written in Greek and Aramaic. The Greek and Aramaic inscriptions are found in Kandahar, Afghanistan. The location of the inscription determined the language of the edict. This shows Ashoka did not impose his language throughout the empire. He acknowledged the existence of multiple languages and wanted to speak with his subjects through their language. Even in contemporary times, many nations are trying to impose the language of the majority throughout the country, neglecting the diversity of the nation and the culture of minority groups. Ashoka's vast empire included a wide range of linguistic and cultural groups. To ensure effective communication, Ashoka issued his inscriptions in several languages and scripts, across the diverse empire. Ashoka's use of multiple languages in his edicts shows his commitment to inclusiveness.

In the Kandahar inscription, Ashoka's principles of Dhamma emphasize compassion, charity, truth, purity, and gentleness as essential virtues for personal and societal growth. He considers himself a guide in promoting these values among his subjects, encouraging them to practice ethical behaviour for the betterment of society. Practical expressions of Dhamma include caring for parents, respecting teachers and elders, and showing kindness to Brahmins, monks, the poor, servants, and others dependent on communal care. This showcases that Ashoka wanted to promote unity in society and elimination of class differences in society. This clearly shows the inclusive attitude of Ashoka towards all sections of people in the society.

Ahimsa (non-violence)

The principle of ahimsa (non-violence) is a significant aspect of Ashoka's Dhamma. It led him to propagate kindness and respect toward all forms of life. Ashoka adopted policies of non-violence and compassion that extended to humans, animals, and nature. Major Rock Edict I prohibits animal sacrifice and certain types of events that are likely to include animal killing. Ashoka himself states that the number of animals killed was reduced.

The most important aspects of Ashoka's administration were inclusiveness and reaffirming the principle of nonviolence. His rule was envisioned to be moral and harmonious. After the deadly Kalinga War, Ashoka abandoned war and violence and declared himself an ahimsa disciple, which means he would not harm any human or other living forms. This combination of inclusivity and nonviolence has provided stability to his kingdom and exemplifies humility and regard for individuals and their diversity in leadership.

Social Welfare

Rock Edict II refers to some of the policies of Ashoka which can be referred to as social welfare policies in contemporary times. Ashoka made provisions for the medical treatment of humans and animals. He encouraged the planting of beneficial medicinal herbs. Ashoka constructed roads, dug wells, and built rest houses for travellers and traders. He also planted trees on both sides of the roads to provide shade for travellers.

Ashoka emphasized good conduct and social responsibilities as key aspects of his Dhamma policy. He also worked to promote the welfare and happiness of servants, masters, traders, farmers, Brahmanas, prisoners, the aged, the destitute, and the elderly. Ashoka asked for courtesy towards slaves and servants, respectful behaviour, and obedience towards elders, mothers, and fathers. All this can be seen in Rock Edicts III, IX, XI, and XII. Ashoka took care of the welfare of the people in his empire, irrespective of their social background or class.

Due to the policy of Dhamma, Ashoka states in Rock Edict IV that aggression, violence, inappropriate behavior toward friends, relatives, and others, along with similar wrongdoings, were controlled and regulated. These things have been done for not just the benefit of humans but also for the benefit of animals. It is a radically different attitude from how the king is portrayed in Arthashastra. Upinder Singh suggests that Ashoka must have considered this as the dhamma of the king.

Protection of Environment

Ashoka is recognized for his promotion of ecological awareness and environmental ethics. His proclamations and edicts mirror his devotion to the conservation of wildlife and the balance of ecology. He prohibited animal sacrifices, limited hunting, and created protected areas for animals. In Pillar Edict V, Ashoka announced protections for certain species and promoted the welfare of animals throughout his empire.

Ashoka encouraged the planting of trees along roadsides, a policy aimed at improving the environment and providing shade for travellers, as well as benefiting animal habitats. He encouraged the cultivation of medicinal plants across his empire. He instructed that herb useful for human and animal medicine be grown in suitable locations, indicating his awareness of biodiversity's role in public health. His edicts mention that Ashoka established centres for medical treatment for both humans and animals, a unique initiative for that time.

Ashoka's ecological consciousness, especially as recorded in his edicts, was quite advanced for his time and reflects a philosophy of respect for nature.

Role of Dhamma Mahamattas

Thirteen years after his coronation, Ashoka established a special group of officials known as Dhamma Mahamatas. In Pillar Edict IV, he describes them as officials tasked with promoting moral values. Their duties included ensuring the welfare and happiness of servants, masters, traders, farmers, Brahmanas, prisoners, the elderly, the destitute, and even the King's relatives. These different categories of people indicate how Ashoka wanted to look after the welfare of people irrespective of class, or background. This clearly shows the inclusive attitude of Ashoka as an emperor. Dhamma Mahamatas had to oversee the welfare of animals as well. They were tasked with fostering kindness and monitoring the humane treatment of all living beings. The activities such as the establishment of veterinary clinics and the planting of medicinal herbs for both humans and animals, are overseen by these officials.

Also, the dhamma mahamatras were instructed to treat the Sangha (Buddhist), the Brahmanas, the Ajivikas, and the Nirgranthas (Jainas) with equal respect (Pillar Edict VII). This clearly shows that even though Ashoka embraced Buddhism he did not wanted to force it among his subjects. He preferred the coexistence of different religious beliefs in his kingdom. Ashoka's establishment of the Dhamma mahamatras effectively demonstrates that Ashoka's Dhamma did not support any specific belief system.

Dhamma mahamatras were instructed to present their reports to the ruler at any moment, regardless of his current activities. This indicates that Ashoka gave preference to fulfilling the duties as a king and catering to the needs of the people. Another example of his inclusive attitude.

Dhamma-yatas

According to Rock Edict VII, the emperor will carry out dhamma-yatas. Previously, the emperor went on leisure travels that included hunting and other pleasures. Dhammayatas supplanted the royal pleasure excursions. It enabled the emperor to come into contact with different kinds of people. He did not isolate himself from the people while being the head of the empire. He wanted to interact with people.

CONCLUSION

According to Romila Thapar, Ashoka's adoption of Dhamma as a state policy was to unify a culturally and religiously diverse empire. The inclusiveness of Ashoka is the cornerstone of his legacy, representing his transition from conqueror to compassionate ruler. Ashoka generated respect of all religions by proclaiming Dhamma, by promoting social egalitarianism, by planning welfare policies for all sections of society, including animals. He issued his edicts in many languages, including Prakrit, Greek, and Aramaic, for communicating his ethical vision to different social and ethnic groups. The ideals of governance advocated by Ashoka, based on non-violence included tolerance and compassion, unified his large empire, and left behind an enduring legacy of inclusive leadership.

REFERENCES

i. Chakravarti, Ranabir. 2016. 'Exploring early India up to c.AD 1300'. New Delhi: Primus Books.

ii. Sharma, Ram S. 2009. 'India's Ancient Past'. New Delhi: Oxford University Press.

iii. Singh, Upinder. 2008. 'A History of Ancient and Early Medieval India: From the Stone Age to the 12th Century'. Pearson Education India.

iv. Thapar, Romila. 2012. 'Ashoka and the Decline of the Mauryas'. Oxford University Press.

3. Inclusiveness through the Art Forms in India

Ms. Gayathri. K
II MA History, Madras Christian College, Chennai

INTRODUCTION

Tribal and folk art forms are powerful symbols of inclusivity in India, a nation known for its enormous cultural diversity. They provide a singular window into the customs, beliefs, and histories of marginalized and indigenous populations. In addition to being creative expressions, these art forms—which have their roots in rural and tribal India—are essential instruments for social change, economic development, and cultural preservation. These customs promote a greater awareness and respect of the various identities that coexist in the country through elaborate paintings, colorful textiles, passionate music, and rhythmic dance. Even though many of these artistic disciplines have been around for millennia, they are frequently underrepresented in popular culture.

Tribal and folk art, on the other hand, have emerged as significant platforms for inclusivity as a result of growing initiatives to support and honor these artistic manifestations; they preserve indigenous knowledge, elevate underrepresented voices, and foster cross-cultural communication. These art forms offer a forum for social cohesion by bridging the divide between traditional and contemporary, rural and urban, enabling varied populations to interact, exchange, and prosper together. In a world that is changing quickly, India's efforts to promote and revive tribal and folk art are not only protecting cultural heritage but also opening the door to a society that is more equal and inclusive.

METHODOLOGY

A qualitative examination of the body of current literature will be the main component of the methodology used to investigate inclusivity through Indian tribal and folk arts. In order to examine the research on tribal and folk arts and its social, cultural, and political significance, a thorough literature survey was carried out.

Secondary sources of information include academic publications that examine inclusivity in Indian art forms. This will involve a thorough analysis of scholarly works on tribal and folk arts, including books, reports, and articles, with an emphasis on how these arts support societal cohesiveness, inclusivity, and the preservation of indigenous cultures. To find important ideas, patterns, and theoretical frameworks pertaining to the cultural importance of different art forms in Indian society, the literature will be subjected to a theme analysis. The study intends to demonstrate how tribal and folk arts support societal integration and the portrayal of underrepresented communities.

FINDINGS

Tribal and folk art contribute to Indian art overall. For many years, it has been transformed. They have changed since the time of classical art. Both tribal and folk art have a native character and are associated with people from various social groupings. The visual arts include paintings that portray their culture, customs, and way of life. This phenomenon is local, and they are the ones closest to nature. Their belief systems enable individuals to perceive things in ways that are unique to them, and this has an impact on their creativity as well. Fairs, festivals, regional deities, and fantasy are all portrayed in tribal and folk art. This portion, which has a mysterious and regional air, cannot be eliminated by Indian art. Tribal and folk art are likewise deeply rooted in nomadic lifestyles. The three main tribal and folk art traditions in India that I have examined in this research study are Warli, Madhubani, and Pithora paintings.

Certain shapes, such as squares, triangles, and circles, were used in Warli paintings to represent various natural components. Another excellent example of Indian tribal art is the Pithora paintings created by the Rathwa, Bhills, and Nayka tribes in Gujarat and Madhya Pradesh. The community's delight and celebration are captured in these paintings. Madhubani paintings feature colorful, dynamic deities, most popularly Krishna and his beloved Radha, and many stories linked with their legend. Their name comes from the village where they were born.

The word "tribal art" refers to the artwork and performances created by various tribes. Tribes in India have distinct forms of artistic expression. Factors such as geography, sociology, history, and customs influence how primitive a tribe is. Positive themes and concepts like birth, life, harvest, voyage, celebration, or marriage are constantly present in Indian tribal art. The Warli culture, whose paintings are based on the idea of Mother Nature, demonstrates how the Indian tribes honor Mother Earth and its essential components. Life and inventiveness are combined in this indigenous art form. Indian tribal sculptures and paintings are records of their cultural heritage and are of a very high caliber.

Tribes have established a niche for themselves in the modern art world. The tribes have the authority and duty to govern and lead them through the art. Men's imaginations are depicted in the symbols, and these imaginations are the feelings that are typical of a certain time and civilization. Different painting techniques and color palettes are used in each culture. In Madhubani paintings, vivid colors, geometric patterns, and stylized figures are used instead of the typical Warli color scheme of white and brown, which depicts men and women with two inverted triangles linked at the points to symbolize the torso and pelvis parts. The first step in the Pithora painting method is Lipai, or background setting with stark red or sometimes white or creme; these reflect the co-existence of hope and despair in the tribal lives. And these paintings are characterized by lucky and sacred symbols like the sun, moon, and horses, and are painted in stunning and bright reds, greens, oranges, blues, and pinks.

Life and creativity are inextricably linked in Indian tribal art. Tribal arts in India are very sensitive. Their passion and mystery are captured in their art, which is an expression of their lives. One of thc most intriguing aspects of Indian tribal culture is tribal art. Tribal arts are a priceless asset that are incredibly diverse, beautiful, and varied. The timeless charm of Indian tribal life is attempted to be fully recreated in traditional tribal art. Beautiful examples of Indian tribal art are readily found throughout the country. Tribal art in India is a live art style that is very expressive and adaptable to the times. It is now an essential component of the nation's culture. The Indian tribes make serious attempts to preserve a thousand-year-old culture that includes art, music, customs, and ceremonies.

By conserving their resources and assimilating into the surroundings, they live in perfect harmony with nature. Indian tribal and folk communities have a strong bond with the environment, which is reflected in the range of natural and locally produced materials they utilize to create their paintings. Vibrant colors are frequently produced using natural pigments made from minerals, plants, and organic materials such as red ochre, charcoal, clay, and turmeric. Water, animal fat, or plant sap are frequently combined with these pigments. While some painters use their fingers or natural tools like leaves and fabric, the brushes are usually handcrafted from twigs, bamboo, or animal hair. Depending on the society and the art style, paintings are typically made on surfaces including walls, cloth, wood, paper, or even clay. For texture and decoration, additional natural elements such as plant fibers, seeds, leaves, and animal bones may be used, which reflects these societies' resourcefulness and sustainability. Indian tribal art has been influenced by modern art, and its narrative style is largely owed to the history of tribal art, which cannot be erased.

Warli Paintings

The northern Sahyadri range in Maharashtra is home to these kinds of artwork. The idea of "Mother Nature" is central to Warli culture. The population relied heavily on farming as their primary source of income and subsistence.

Using their clay homes as a canvas, the Warli people paint using geometric forms that represent various natural components, such as squares, triangles, and circles. The square appears to be a man-made design that denotes a sacred enclosure or a plot of land, the triangle shows mountains, conical figures, and trees, and the circle represents the moon and sun.

The colors used in Warli paintings are typically brown and white. Each ritual painting's main subject is a square-like structure known as Chauk or Chaukat. Chauk comes in two varieties: Devchauk and Lagnachauk. Palghat, a mother goddess, is portrayed inside a Devchauk. She is revered as the fraternity goddess.

In these paintings, male gods are uncommon and usually associated with spirits that have assumed human forms. Hunting, fishing, and farming scenes, as well as the representation of forests and animals, are the main subjects. In these paintings, we might also see scenes of festivals, dances, and daily activities.

The "Tarpa dance," which is a trumpet-like instrument, is one of the main themes that is portrayed in numerous artworks. A human body would be constructed from two inverse triangles, with the lower triangle representing the pelvis and the upper triangle representing the torso. The figure is a man if the top triangle is larger than the lower triangle, and a lady if the bottom triangle is broader than the upper.

The paintings often employ a red ochre background and are made on the interior walls of village homes. Branches, mud, and brick are mixed to create this color. White pigment, which is formed by mixing rice flour and water and employing gum as a binder, is the only color applied to this background. It's fascinating that they chewed on a bamboo stick to simulate the texture of a paintbrush. Only on special occasions are the walls painted, and this style of painting is still used today.

Madhubani Paintings

In the Mithila region of Bihar, India, Madhubani paintings are a hit. This is more of a form of folk art. They employ vibrant colors, geometric designs, stylized motifs, and natural dyes. The Madhubani paintings are used to depict religious tales and adorn walls, floors, and furniture. These paintings, which were usually made by women in the Mithila region, were also referred to as Mithila paintings.

Behind these artworks lies a history. According to legend, the designs were commissioned by Janaka, the ruler of Mithila, to illustrate his daughter Sita's wedding during the Ramayana period. So this artwork came into being. Interestingly, however, it wasn't until 1934 that William

G. Archer, a British colonial commander, found this artwork. This invites the question of why this artwork, which is claimed to have originated during the epic period, was only discovered in a later period. One of the primary causes of this is that the artwork was made on soil grounds or mud walls during auspicious occasions and then removed the following day, so that it is not preserved.

Women were encouraged to paint on canvas, paper, or fabric in order to make a living during a severe drought and spread this art form around the world. The designs are created using matchsticks, twigs, and even fingers. These paintings are characterized by line drawings that are full of vividly contrasting colors and patterns, and they can be little or enormous.

To depict various eras and locations, the paintings are separated into portions that are both horizontal and vertical. The intricate mathematical patterns gave the hues their charm and individuality, even though they were created entirely of natural materials.

Gods' and goddesses' bodies are frequently truncated and deformed. Images of Radha Krishna, Ganesha, and Rama Lakshmana Seetha are classical examples. The eyes are painted in frontal view, while the faces are displayed in profile. The eyes are thought to often be painted last. Fish, lotus flowers, peacocks, the sun, moon, elephants, snakes, tigers, mango trees, crows, and so on were among the important symbols.

Pithora Paintings

These paintings resemble indigenous art more. These were painted on the walls by the tribes of Rathwa, Bhils, and Bhilala.The rock art, the wall, and the cave were those. The paintings are created in honor of a tribal goddess known as Baba Pithora, and the local gods are also honored.

Males known as "Lakhindra" were typically the painters. Since women are viewed as unclean due to their menstruation, they were either barred from or restricted from participating in the painting process. However, using dung, water, and chuna, the unmarried girls assisted in plastering the walls' backdrop. All things considered, this is a male-centric practice, and the head priest is also involved.

"Lipai," or background setup, is the first step in the painting process. The background is painted in vibrant and striking shades of red, green, orange, blue, and pink. Horses, the sun, and the moon were among the fortunate and revered mascots that set the paintings apart. There are also trees, birds, animals, etc. The everyday occupations of the rural populace were exquisitely portrayed in these paintings. The fact that no two paintings are ever alike is a crucial aspect that serves as the artists' distinctive selling factor. In addition to providing a white or cream background, they can also locate a bold red background that appeals to modern preferences in rustic mud colors. These illustrate how hope and sorrow coexist in tribal life.

Through their representation of the various cultures, customs, and histories of India's indigenous and rural populations, tribal and folk art forms are crucial in fostering inclusivity in the nation. India is home to a diverse range of tribal communities, each of which has its own distinctive artistic traditions that are a reflection of its way of life, values, and interaction with the natural world. By integrating these frequently neglected communities into the mainstream, these art forms not only highlight the variety of Indian society but also promote a sense of inclusivity and unity. Here's how tribal and folk art forms in India promote inclusiveness:

Celebrating Diversity and Cultural Identity

Tribal and folk art styles in India are intricately linked to the cultural identities of different groups. Underrepresented populations, especially tribal societies, can convey their own worldviews, customs, and social structures through these creative forms. They foster a deeper appreciation and respect for the variety inside Indian society by using art to showcase various customs. For instance, one of India's most well-known tribal art forms is the Warli paintings of Maharashtra, which were produced by the Warli tribe. They use basic geometric designs to represent nature, daily life, and spiritual ideas. These pieces of art, which are currently on exhibit in galleries and exhibitions, give the Warli people visibility and enable others to recognize the depth of their culture.

Preservation and Promotion of Heritage

In India, folk and tribal art forms are essential for conserving the cultural heritage of groups that are frequently marginalized. In order to maintain continuity and a link to the past, many of these artistic disciplines are handed down through the generations. India is able to preserve its cultural legacy by supporting these art forms, which in turn promotes inclusion by making these customs available to individuals from many backgrounds.

Economic Empowerment through Art

For underprivileged communities, tribal and folk art can be a source of economic emancipation. These art forms give artisans—many of them are from indigenous or tribal groups—a living by becoming well-known on a local, national, and worldwide scale. By uplifting these communities, this economic empowerment promotes greater social and economic inclusivity.

Art as a Platform for Social and Political Advocacy

In India, tribal and folk artists frequently utilize their work to remark on social and political issues. They give underprivileged people a voice and increase awareness by drawing attention to issues including environmental degradation, land rights, and cultural survival. Because it questions prevailing narratives and draws attention to the hardships of tribal and indigenous peoples, this is a potent instrument for inclusivity.

Bridging the Urban-Rural Divide

In India, where industrialization and urbanization have occasionally resulted in the marginalization of rural and tribal groups, tribal and folk art act as a link between the two. There is a chance to promote a better awareness and respect of rural and tribal customs by exhibiting these art forms in metropolitan venues including galleries, museums, and cultural festivals. This also makes it easier for urban dwellers to comprehend the difficulties and complexities that tribal societies experience.

Incorporating Tribal and Folk Art into Contemporary Art

Tribal and folk themes have been included into the works of several modern Indian artists, contributing to the popularization of these art forms. By doing this, they offer tribal and folk art a contemporary relevance while simultaneously honoring traditional aesthetics. This openness promotes communication between traditional and modern creative forms as well as cross-cultural exchange.

For instance, modern artists and designers all around the world have adopted the Bihar folk art form known as Madhubani paintings. More awareness and admiration of this tribal art style as well as acceptance within the larger Indian cultural scene have resulted from the adaptation of Madhubani art's elaborate, colorful patterns into contemporary contexts including fashion, digital art, and interior design.

Creating Opportunities for Tribal Women

Women have traditionally been the main keepers of creative heritage in many indigenous cultures. Women can express their creativity, maintain their traditional customs, and make money through tribal and folk art. By strengthening women in a country where they may have historically had little chances, this advances gender inclusion. The Madhubani paintings are a famous example; women in the Mithila region were usually the ones who made them.

Fostering Unity Through Collective Celebration

The communal aspect of many tribal and folk art forms promotes group engagement and the exchange of artistic heritage. Folk and tribal art-focused festivals, fairs, and cultural events provide venues for individuals from various origins to mingle, celebrate, and learn about one another's customs.

CONCLUSION

In conclusion, by overcoming geographical, social, and cultural barriers, tribal and folk art forms in India are essential to promoting inclusivity. In addition to preserving the various cultural identities of disenfranchised people, these centuries-old art forms foster social cohesiveness and a sense of belonging. These art forms provide a special forum for the expression of indigenous worldviews and societal values through their use of natural materials, unique techniques, and narrative. We may better understand India's rich cultural legacy by participating in these artistic endeavors, which emphasizes the value of inclusivity and cultural preservation in modern society. Ultimately, a more welcoming and peaceful society where different viewpoints are valued and acknowledged can be greatly aided by the ongoing acknowledgment and encouragement of tribal and folk art forms.

APPENDIX

Warli Painting

Madhubani Painting

Pithora Painting

REFERENCES

i. Satyawadi, Sudha.2010. 'Unique Art of Warli Paintings'. DK Print world. Bhal, Sushma.2015. 'Madhubani

ii. Art. Museum of Sacred Art. Wolf, Gita. 2019. 'Painting Everything in the World'. Tara books.

iii. Moodie, Megan. 2015. 'We were Adivasis'. University of Chicago Press.

4. Dialogue on Gender, Social Justice and Inclusiveness: A Field Perspective on Policies for Social Inclusion and Equity

Dr. Karunya Devi. N

Social Worker, Advocate & Member, Child Welfare Committee, North Chennai

INTRODUCTION

The need for social inclusion, gender justice, and equity in marginalized communities is critical, particularly within child protection systems. The Protection of Children from Sexual Offences (POCSO) Act plays a central role in safeguarding vulnerable children in India. However, while the policy exists, its effectiveness is often hindered by systemic gaps in implementation. The lack of coordination and awareness across various sectors—police, judiciary, and educational institutions—compromises the delivery of justice and support to POCSO survivors, especially those from marginalized backgrounds.

This paper analyzes the intersection of child protection systems and marginalized communities, drawing from the field experiences of a Child Welfare Committee (CWC) member in Tamil Nadu. By examining the practical challenges and discrepancies in policy application, the paper critiques existing structures that hinder the POCSO Act's intended outcomes. Specifically, the failure to prioritize education for survivors, coupled with insufficient awareness within key institutions, limits the potential for social inclusion and equity. This paper explores how the principles Compassion and Equity can inform and improve child protection systems. Through an analytical review, the paper advocates for policy shifts, including the prioritization of education for POCSO survivors, institutional awareness programs, and the role of youth advocates in fostering social change.

Theoretical Framework: Social Justice and Child Protection

This paper is grounded in the principles of social justice and child protection. Social justice in the context of child protection ensures that all children, regardless of their background, have equal access to protection, opportunities, and support. Gender justice ensures that the POCSO Act is applied equitably, ensuring both boys and girls benefit from its protective provisions.

Legal and Institutional Framework: The POCSO Act and its Implementation:

The POCSO Act is a pivotal piece of legislation designed to safeguard children from sexual offenses in India, but its implementation faces significant challenges, particularly in marginalized communities. Studies have shown that while the Act is comprehensive, systemic barriers such as lack of coordination and awareness among the police, judiciary, and educational institutions continue to impede its effectiveness. These gaps delay justice and support for survivors, particularly those from underprivileged backgrounds (National Commission for Protection of Child Rights [NCPCR], 2018).

Educational access remains a significant challenge for POCSO survivors, who often face institutional and societal barriers. While Saraswathy, D. (2024) advocates for fee waivers and priority admissions to enhance access to higher education for POCSO survivors, many educational institutions lack the infrastructure to fully support these initiatives, thereby perpetuating inequality.

Analytical Framework: Gaps in Coordination

The coordination gaps among key stakeholders—police, Child Welfare Committees (CWC), judiciary, and educational institutions—significantly hinder the effectiveness of child protection systems. Training deficits among law enforcement and judicial officers exacerbate these gaps, often resulting in mishandling of cases, insensitive questioning, or delayed interventions. As Susanth (2024) highlights, these barriers lead to compromised outcomes for survivors, slowing their reintegration into society and preventing full social inclusion.

METHODOLOGY

This paper employs a qualitative research methodology, grounded in the field experience of a Child Welfare Committee (CWC) member in Tamil

Nadu, focusing on the POCSO Act. The research is exploratory, relying on experiential data derived from direct involvement with marginalized communities and the child protection system.

The CWC member's first hand exposure to cases involving POCSO survivors provides a rich, contextual understanding of the systemic challenges and barriers faced by these communities. Instead of traditional sampling techniques or case studies, the study draws on observational data and in-depth personal accounts to analyze the intersection of gender justice, social equity, and child protection policies. Through case documentation, discussions with stakeholders, and detailed narratives, the paper examines the practical implications of policy implementation and identifies gaps in institutional awareness and coordination among key players in the child protection system—namely the police, judiciary, and educational institutions. An analytical approach is employed to evaluate the effectiveness of these policies, with particular attention to how systemic failures in awareness and coordination negatively affect the support systems available to marginalized children. The paper highlights areas where youth-led advocacy and community mobilization can serve as key drivers of social change, furthering the cause of gender justice and social equity in Tamil Nadu.

FINDINGS AND THEMATIC ANALYSIS

This thematic analysis explores the various factors impacting marginalized children within the child protection system, particularly those affected by the POCSO Act. Through the experiences of a Child Welfare Committee (CWC) member in Tamil Nadu, several critical themes emerge, highlighting the systemic, gender-related, and institutional challenges faced by survivors of sexual abuse.

1. Systemic Gaps in Awareness and Coordination

A significant theme emerging from the field analysis is the lack of awareness and coordination across key stakeholders, including the police, judiciary, and educational institutions. Many officers, whether in law enforcement or social services, lack the specialized training needed to handle sensitive cases under the POCSO Act. This leads to miscommunication, delays, and insufficient responses to child sexual abuse cases.

Empirical Example: A young survivor, after being rescued from an abusive situation, faced delays in the judicial process due to poor coordination between the police and the CWC. Each department had different sets of protocols, resulting in confusion and further delays in addressing her case. This case exemplifies how fragmented services can compromise a survivor's access to timely support and justice. A lack of follow-up and poor communication between sectors further prolonged the trauma.

2. Gender Conflicts and Patriarchal Norms

Gender-related biases within the child protection system are another critical issue. These biases manifest in both the gendered responses of male and female officers and the broader institutional structures shaped by patriarchal norms. Female officers often struggle for authority and recognition in predominantly male-dominated spaces such as police and judiciary roles. Meanwhile, male officers may avoid handling cases involving female survivors due to ingrained gender stereotypes.

Empirical Example: In one instance, a young girl who had experienced severe physical abuse by her mother was initially met with skepticism from a male officer, who questioned her credibility based on societal assumptions about women's roles in the family. The female social worker, advocating for the child's rights, faced pushback from the male officer, which delayed the case's progress. This story underscores the gendered challenges that survivors face, not just from their abusers but from the very systems designed to protect them.

3. Barriers to Accessing Education for POCSO Survivors

Education plays a crucial role in the recovery and social integration of survivors of sexual abuse. However, POCSO survivors, especially those from marginalized communities, face significant barriers to accessing education. Survivors, particularly girls, may not return to school due to stigmatization and fear of being ostracized. Some schools, especially in rural areas, may refuse to admit survivors or fail to provide the necessary support services.

Empirical Example: A young girl who was rescued from a trafficker faced rejection from several schools in her community due to the stigma attached to her past. Financial barriers also made it impossible for her to continue her education, as her family could not afford the school fees. Despite provisions in the POCSO Act for fee waivers and priority admission, the lack of awareness about these rights in local institutions prevented her from accessing education. It was only after advocacy from social workers that she was finally admitted to a school with the necessary support services.

4. Lack of Legal Support and Delays in Justice

The delays in the judicial process contribute to extended trauma for survivors of sexual violence. Although the POCSO Act mandates swift and specialized handling of cases, delays in investigations, court proceedings, and poor documentation prolong the trauma for survivors.

Empirical Example: In a case involving a young survivor of sexual abuse, the legal proceedings were delayed due to bureaucratic inefficiencies and lack of training among the legal staff on handling sensitive cases. The survivor, already coping with the trauma of abuse, was forced to wait for months before her case was properly heard in court, exacerbating her emotional distress. This case highlights how delays in justice can lead to re-traumatization of survivors and how urgent reforms in the legal system are necessary to address these issues.

5. Inconsistent Implementation of POCSO Provisions

Another key theme is the inconsistent implementation of provisions under the POCSO Act. Despite the Act mandating specific measures to protect survivors, their application is not uniform across regions. Many districts suffer from a lack of awareness or inadequate training among local authorities, leading to inequitable treatment of survivors.

Empirical Example: A survivor from a rural community faced significant challenges in accessing the provisions of the POCSO Act. The local

Child Welfare Committee was not aware of the available services under the Act, and the survivor's case was mishandled. It was only after the involvement of higher authorities that the proper procedures were followed. This case underscores the need for standardized training across regions to ensure that all survivors are treated fairly and in accordance with the law.

6. Role of Youth-Led Advocacy and Awareness

Youth-led advocacy is identified as a pivotal factor in promoting social inclusion and gender justice. College students and youth activists can serve as key drivers of change, advocating for better institutional responses, educational reform, and greater awareness of the rights of marginalized children.

RECOMMENDATIONS

Strengthening Support and Awareness for POCSO Survivors: A Comprehensive Approach

The government's efforts to support POCSO (Protection of Children from Sexual Offences) survivors should focus on a multi-faceted approach that enhances education, strengthens legal processes, promotes gender equity, and creates a supportive community environment.

1. Strengthening Interdepartmental Coordination and Collaboration

To ensure seamless support for POCSO survivors, the government should foster stronger interdepartmental coordination. This can be achieved by:

Unified Child Protection Protocols: Create clear communication channels and defined roles across departments (police, judiciary, educational institutions, CWCs) to avoid delays or overlap in handling cases.

Cross-Departmental Workshops: Conduct joint task force workshops that bring together stakeholders to share insights, discuss case complexities, and streamline responses to POCSO cases.

Digital Platforms for Case Tracking: Implement digital systems for tracking case progress and sharing information across departments to ensure no case is overlooked.

2. Comprehensive Training for Key Stakeholders

The effectiveness of child protection efforts hinges on well-trained professionals. Therefore, the government should prioritize the following:

Trauma-Informed Care: Offer ongoing trauma-informed care training to police officers, educators, judicial staff, and CWC members to ensure they handle sensitive cases with empathy and care.

Gender Sensitivity Training: Address gender biases through mandatory gender sensitivity programs, ensuring professionals are equipped to handle gender-related challenges within the system.

Legal Literacy on POCSO: Regularly update training programs to ensure professionals are fully aware of the legal provisions of the POCSO Act, including the rights and protections afforded to survivors.

3. Enhanced Access to Education and Support Services for Survivors

To address the educational barriers faced by POCSO survivors, the following interventions are essential:

Admission and Support in Higher Education: Issue directives prioritizing POCSO survivors for admissions in government colleges, coupled with fee waivers and specialized support programs.

Specialized Programs for Survivors: Establish counseling, mentorship, and academic support programs in schools to address both the psychological needs and educational requirements of POCSO survivors.

Community Awareness Campaigns: Educate parents and children about their rights, including access to education, financial support, and legal assistance, to help them navigate the systems available for survivors.

4. Promoting Gender Equity in Social Work Practices

The protection of survivors must be grounded in a gender-sensitive approach. To achieve this:

Gender-Neutral Language and Practices: Introduce gender-neutral language and practices within child welfare services to ensure that all stakeholders, regardless of gender, can handle sensitive cases without bias.

Incorporation of Gender Studies: Integrate gender studies into the training of all child protection professionals to challenge patriarchal norms and promote equitable treatment of all survivors.

Gender Equity Assessments: Regularly assess child welfare institutions for gender equity, ensuring that their policies and practices do not inadvertently reinforce discrimination.

5. Youth-led advocacy and Empowerment Initiatives

College students and young activists can play a pivotal role in promoting child protection and supporting POCSO survivors. The government can facilitate youth engagement through the following:

Peer-to-Peer Education: Establish youth-led programs that educate peers on gender equality, child protection, and the importance of the POCSO Act, empowering the next generation to advocate for social justice.

Youth Advocacy Programs: Create platforms for young leaders to engage in policy discussions, raise awareness in communities, and advocate for stronger implementation of child protection laws.

Student Volunteer Programs: Encourage college students, particularly those in social work and law, to volunteer with CWCs and NGOs, gaining hands-on experience in child protection efforts.

6. Policy and Legal Reforms for Timely Justice

Ensuring timely justice for survivors is essential. The following reforms should be prioritized:

Fast-Track Courts: Establish special fast-track courts dedicated to POCSO cases, ensuring quicker resolution and reducing the emotional toll on survivors.

Judicial Audits and Assessments: Regular audits of the judicial process will help identify bottlenecks and inefficiencies, followed by corrective measures to expedite the legal proceedings.

Public Awareness Campaigns: Increase public awareness of the POCSO Act, empowering communities to understand their rights and advocate for timely justice.

7. Community Engagement and Support Systems for Survivors

Community involvement is critical in providing a safe, supportive environment for POCSO survivors. The government can strengthen this through:

Community-Based Support Groups: Establish survivor support groups in local communities to help survivors and their families reintegrate, provide emotional support, and reduce stigma.

Collaborative Efforts with Local Leaders: Engage local religious, community, and political leaders to spread awareness and advocate for the protection of children, leveraging their influence to drive cultural change.

Grassroots Awareness Campaigns: Launch community-level campaigns to educate the public on child protection, ensuring that everyone is aware of the reporting mechanisms and their role in protecting children.

8. Research and Innovation in Child Protection

Investing in research will help improve the effectiveness of child protection efforts. Key initiatives include:

Research on POCSO Implementation: Conduct studies on the effectiveness of current child protection systems, identifying best practices and areas for improvement.

Innovation Competitions for Child Safety: Host competitions in colleges and universities to develop innovative solutions, such as apps for anonymous reporting or educational tools for awareness, tailored to the local context.

CONCLUSION

The recommendations provided in this paper are not merely technical fixes; they are aligned with the deeper values of compassion and equity drawn from Buddhist heritage. Each recommendation—from comprehensive training for stakeholders to youth-led advocacy—is designed to address the systemic gaps identified, such as the lack of coordination, inadequate training, and educational barriers faced by POCSO survivors. These gaps undermine the effectiveness of the child protection system, particularly for marginalized children. By focusing on trauma-informed care, gender sensitivity, and the prioritization of education, the recommendations aim to create a supportive environment where all children, regardless of their background, have equal access to justice and protection.

Equity and Compassion these principles emphasize the interconnectedness of all individuals and the need for compassion in addressing social issues. This perspective aligns with the need for an integrated child protection system that values empathy, collective responsibility, and the well-being of every child. The recommendations advocate for a child-centric approach, ensuring that systemic responses are both compassionate and efficient. By fostering community engagement, encouraging youth advocacy, and integrating gender equity into training, the proposed changes envision a holistic transformation. This vision is not only about correcting institutional flaws but about building a society where marginalized children are not just protected but are allowed to thrive with dignity and support, reflecting a just and inclusive social order.

REFERENCES

National Commission for Protection of Child Rights. (2018). POCSO Act and its implementation challenges in India. https://www.ncpcr.gov.in

Susanth, N., & Santhosh, M. (2024). A study on the impact of the POCSO Act and its challenges concerning Indian society. International Journal of Advanced Research in Science, Communication, and Technology, 4(2). https://ijarsct.co.in/Paper17912.pdf

Saraswathy, D. (2024). Challenges in child rights and child protection in India. International Journal of Justice, Social and Regulatory Studies, 1(1). https://researchjournal.org.in/index.php/ijjsrs/article/view/35/12

5. Promoting Social Inclusion through Employment: Assessing the Socio- Economic Impact of MGNREGA in Rural Communities of Chengalpattu

Ms. Tharani. T, Assistant Professor, Social Work, SDNB Vaishnav College
Mr. Jacob Steyns, II MSW & Dr. S. Sudharsan, Assistant Professor
Department of Social Work, Madras Christian College, Chennai

INTRODUCTION

The Mahatma Gandhi National Rural Employment Guarantee Act (MGNREGA), launched in 2005, represents one of the largest social protection initiatives in India. It aims to provide a safety net for rural households by guaranteeing 100 days of wage employment annually, with a focus on alleviating poverty, reducing unemployment, and promoting social inclusion. MGNREGA is unique in its design, as it targets the most marginalized sections of society, including women, scheduled castes, and scheduled tribes, ensuring that they have access to employment and livelihood opportunities. In rural areas, where agriculture and allied activities are often unreliable sources of income, MGNREGA has emerged as a vital mechanism for financial security. It not only guarantees employment but also contributes to the creation of rural infrastructure, such as roads, water conservation systems, and community assets, which enhances the overall quality of life for rural residents. Furthermore, the scheme fosters social inclusion by actively involving marginalized communities in the planning, execution, and monitoring of projects.

Review of Literature

The Mahatma Gandhi National Rural Employment Guarantee Act (MGNREGA), launched in 2005, aims to alleviate rural poverty by providing 100 days of paid employment for rural households. The scheme aims to strengthen the livelihood base of the poor and to proactively ensure social inclusion. Studies have highlighted its significant impact on improving the participation of marginalized groups. The scheme promoting women empowerment has led to a significant increase in the engagement of women in paid employment, especially in public works (Chaudhury et.al, 2012). Women's Financial Independence and their Decision-making power within households has also seen a notable increase (Agarwal, 2008).

MGNREGA has also played an important role in decreasing caste discrimination and promoting economic inclusion for Scheduled Castes (SCs) and Scheduled Tribes. According to Dutta (2013), the program has helped historically marginalized groups by giving them access to previously unattainable paid employment. Desai and Namboodiri (2017), agree that MGNREGA has created an inclusive labor market in rural India, but caste-based discrimination still prevents these populations from fully integrating into work environments. By providing an income stream to groups traditionally excluded from economic opportunities, MGNREGA has helped reduce rural social and economic disparities.

Despite these successes, challenges in the implementation of MGNREGA persist. Mishra and Soni (2015) highlight delays in wage payments, corruption, and bureaucratic inefficiencies, which undermine the program's potential to fully foster social inclusion. Sen (2014) further points out that the physical nature of the work, along with low wages, limits MGNREGA's effectiveness in improving the quality of life for workers in the long run. In conclusion, while MGNREGA has had a positive impact on reducing rural poverty and promoting social inclusion, addressing its implementation challenges is crucial for maximizing its potential benefits.

METHODOLOGY

The study employed a mixed-method approach to explore the socio-economic impacts of the MGNREGA scheme in Chengalpattu, combining both quantitative and qualitative data to provide a comprehensive understanding of its effects. For the quantitative component, simple random sampling was used to select 150 beneficiaries from various rural communities. These participants were administered structured questionnaires designed to collect data on key socio-economic indicators such as income generation, livelihood security, women's empowerment, infrastructure development, and social inclusion. To complement the quantitative data, qualitative data was collected through Focused Group Discussions (FGDs) with smaller groups of beneficiaries. These discussions provided deeper insights into the personal experiences and perceptions of the participants regarding the effectiveness of MGNREGA.

FINDINGS

Socio-Demographic Profile

A majority (45%) of the respondents were aged between 31-40, 39% were aged between 41-50 years, 10% were between 21-30 years and 6% above 51 years. The gender distribution is balanced, with an equal split between male and female respondents (50% each). 92% of the respondents were married. The remaining 5% were unmarried and 3% were widower/widow. This marital status distribution suggests that the majority of participants are engaged in family-based livelihoods, and could be seen as an indication of the role of MNREGA in supporting family welfare and promoting economic security for households in rural areas.

A significant portion (52%) of respondents had completed only primary school education, while 12% were illiterate. 20%, 7% and 9% of the respondents have completed their secondary education, SSLC and Higher Secondary respectively.

The majority (80%) of respondents reported working solely under MNREGA, with a significant proportion of respondents were (20%) employed in agricultural works. This reliance on MNREGA as the primary source of income underscores the significance of MNREGA in providing livelihood opportunities to rural populations, many of whom may not have access to more stable or diversified employment.

Increased Income Stability

A significant number of respondents (87%) reported that MGNREGA provided a stable income that helped them meet daily expenses and provided financial support during the off-season of agricultural work.

Most participants (72%) reported that MGNREGA wages made up a substantial portion of their household income. A predominant theme that emerged from the FGD is the Consistent Source of Income. The respondents were mostly dependent on the income provided by MGNREGA. A respondent stated that, "My family relies on this wage. Sometimes, it is the only source of income for us. Even when there are no agricultural works, we get income from this 100 days of work".

Increased Financial Independence among Women

Women, who constituted a significant portion of the study (around 50%), has experienced a boost in financial independence. Among the female respondents, 69% of respondents indicated that MGNREGA wages allowed them to independently manage household expenses and save for emergencies. For many women, this financial autonomy translated into greater decision-making power in household matters, such as child education and healthcare. A female respondent stated that, "I can contribute to my household and even help my children with their education. This income has given me confidence I never had before."

Access to Banking Services

All the respondents (100%) had a bank account in which the salary was credited. Among this, 80% of the respondents stated that this was their first bank account. Participants who receive their wages through direct bank transfers, highlighted how the scheme facilitated their access to banking services. This shift from cash payments to bank transfers has brought financial inclusion to many rural households. A respondent stated that, "The wages are directly transferred to my bank account through MGNREGA. At first, I wasn't sure about it, but now I see how much easier it is to access my money whenever I need it. I didn't have the need to access bank before, I didn't even have an account. But now I'm able to access banking services on my own. I can draw or deposit cash without any assistance."

Enhanced Participation in Local Governance

86% of respondents participated in the social audits organized as part of the MGNREGA implementation process. Social audits are seen as a significant step towards ensuring transparency and accountability in the management of funds and implementation of projects. Also, 82% of the respondents participated in the Gram Sabha meetings conducted concerning MGNREGA.

The study found that MGNREGA has improved community participation, particularly in decision-making related to local development projects. Many beneficiaries reported increased involvement in the planning and monitoring of MGNREGA projects, which was seen as a step toward greater social inclusion. Rural women and marginalized groups, who were previously excluded from decision-making processes, are now more active in local governance, contributing to a sense of empowerment and ownership.

Infrastructure Development

MGNREGA has led to the construction of significant rural infrastructure, such as roads, water conservation structures, and community assets. Beneficiaries reported improved access to essential services, such as transportation, clean water, and irrigation, which directly contributed to their well-being. 78% of respondents reported that the assets created under MGNREGA, including roads, water tanks, and ponds, were frequently used by the community. These infrastructure assets have had a positive impact on local connectivity and access to essential resources such as water and transportation.

Challenges and Limitations

Delayed Wage Payments: A major challenge for MGNREGA beneficiaries was the frequent delays in wage payments, with 70% of respondents reporting that they often faced delays in receiving their wages. These delays severely impacted the financial stability of rural households, especially for those who rely on MGNREGA wages for their daily needs. A respondent stated that, "Sometimes the wages are delayed for weeks, which makes it hard to manage my expenses. While the work is good, the delay in payments causes stress and uncertainty."

Inadequate Training and Capacity Building: 77% of respondents reported that they had not received any vocational training under the scheme. While the scheme has created employment opportunities, training and skill development were identified as significant gaps. Several beneficiaries, especially women and unskilled laborers, felt that they lacked the necessary training to improve their productivity or shift to higher-paying tasks within the program. This limits the potential for long-term economic mobility.

Inaccurate Beneficiary Identification: A significant issue raised by 15% of respondents was dissatisfaction with the beneficiary identification process. Many individuals, particularly from marginalized communities, felt excluded from the program, with some expressing that the selection process was not transparent and fair. This led to inconsistencies in the program's reach and effectiveness, particularly in marginalized communities

SUGGESTIONS

Community-Based Monitoring and Advocacy Groups

One effective social work intervention would be to establish community-based monitoring and advocacy groups. Social workers can organize and train community members, particularly marginalized groups like women and Scheduled Castes (SCs), to form local committees that can actively monitor the implementation of MGNREGA projects. These committees can oversee the quality of work, ensure timely wage payments, and identify any local corruption or political biases that might affect the program. Social workers can also provide training on how to file complaints and advocate for their rights. For instance, these groups can track wage disbursements, ensure transparency in the allocation of jobs, and alert the government about discrepancies in the program's implementation. This form of grassroots advocacy not only promotes accountability but also empowers community members to actively engage in improving MGNREGA's delivery.

Capacity Building for Local Government Officials

To address issues such as delays in wage payments and inefficient beneficiary identification, social workers could organize capacity-building workshops for local government officials and MGNREGA field staff. These workshops would focus on improving the efficiency of administrative processes, including timely disbursement of wages, accurate beneficiary identification, and transparent selection of workers. Additionally, social workers can assist in integrating digital tools and platforms that help streamline wage payments and beneficiary registration. By offering targeted training to local officials on effective implementation practices, such as ensuring timely payment schedules and maintaining proper records, these interventions would reduce inefficiencies and administrative delays, which currently hinder MGNREGA's potential.

Skill Development and Livelihood Diversification Programs

To overcome the challenge of inadequate training for beneficiaries, a specific social work intervention could be the introduction of skill development programs tailored to local economic conditions and MGNREGA's goals. Social workers can collaborate with vocational training centers, NGOs, and local businesses to offer workshops in marketable skills. Special focus should be placed on creating gender-sensitive programs that empower women by providing them access to skills that traditionally may not have been available to them.

Strengthening Financial Literacy and Access to Financial Services

To address the challenge of financial instability caused by delayed payments, social workers can implement targeted financial literacy programs for MGNREGA beneficiaries. These programs would focus on budgeting, saving, and planning for periods when payments are delayed. Social workers could also facilitate partnerships between banks and local communities to help beneficiaries open accounts and understand how to use banking services effectively. Such initiatives would promote financial inclusion and ensure that wage payments are efficiently managed. Furthermore, social workers can guide beneficiaries in utilizing digital financial tools, including mobile banking, which will help them track their earnings, avoid financial pitfalls, and make informed decisions regarding their household expenses and savings.

CONCLUSION

In conclusion, the Mahatma Gandhi National Rural Employment Guarantee Act (MGNREGA) has proven to be a vital tool in promoting social inclusion, income stability, and community participation in rural areas, particularly in Chengalpattu. The scheme has significantly improved financial independence, especially among women, facilitated access to banking services, and contributed to the development of rural infrastructure. However, challenges such as delayed wage payments, lack of vocational training, and issues with beneficiary identification continue to undermine its effectiveness. Social work interventions, such as community-based monitoring, capacity building for local officials, skill development programs, financial literacy workshops, and improved beneficiary identification processes, can address these challenges. By empowering local communities, enhancing administrative processes, and providing targeted support to marginalized groups, these interventions would further enhance MGNREGA's impact, ensuring that it fulfills its potential in fostering social inclusion and sustainable livelihood opportunities for rural populations.

REFERENCES

1. Agarwal, B. (2008). Gender inequality, empowerment, and the role of MGNREGA. Economic and Political Weekly, 43(18), 25-32.

2. Banerjee, A., et al. (2016). MGNREGA and its effectiveness in rural India. Journal of Social Policy.

3. Bhat, S., & Sundaram, P. (2015). Social security and rural development: A study of MGNREGA. Indian Journal of Rural Development.

4. Bhaduri, A., & Sen, S. (2014). MGNREGA and its impact on rural livelihoods. Economic and Political Weekly, 49(33), 18-21.

5. Chaudhury, S., et al. (2012). Women's participation in MGNREGA and its effects. Economic and Political Weekly, 47(42), 41-46.

6. Das, P., & Singh, S. (2013). Women's empowerment and the MGNREGA. International Journal of Rural Development.

7. Desai, M., & Namboodiri, A. (2017). Social inclusion and MGNREGA: Addressing caste-based exclusion in rural India. Journal of South Asian Development, 12(3), 285-302.

8. Desai, V., & Mishra, S. (2016). MGNREGA and social inclusion: A critical analysis. Indian Journal of Social Work.

9. Dutta, S. (2013). Caste and class in rural India: The role of MGNREGA in economic inclusion. Journal of Rural Development, 32(2), 133-150.

10. Khera, R. (2011). The impact of NREGA on rural employment and poverty in India. Economic & Political Weekly, 46(31), 63-74.

11. Kumar, R. (2015). MGNREGA and rural infrastructure: Enhancing access to services. Indian Journal of Social Science, 19(4), 110-126.

12. Kundu, R., & Pothen, P. (2017). The wage gap in MGNREGA: A gender perspective. Journal of Development Economics.

13. Mishra, S., & Soni, P. (2015). Challenges in the implementation of MGNREGA: A critical analysis. International Journal of Rural Development, 22(2), 47-59.

14. Murgai, R., et al. (2010). MGNREGA and rural poverty alleviation: A preliminary assessment. World Bank Policy Research Working Paper No. 5395.

15. Shah, S. (2019). MGNREGA and social inclusion: A case study from rural Bihar. Indian Journal of Social Work, 80(1), 44-57.

16. Sharma, A., & Gupta, R. (2020). Evaluating the socio-economic impact of MGNREGA on rural livelihoods. Journal of Development Studies, 58(4), 1123-1140.

17. Sivakumar, R. (2014). MGNREGA: Rural employment and its impact. Economic and Political Weekly.

18. Sundaram, K., & Tendulkar, S. D. (2010). The effect of MGNREGA on poverty and the rural economy. Economic and Political Weekly, 45(10), 22-27.

19. World Bank. (2022). India's MGNREGA: Impacts, challenges, and future directions. World Bank Publications.

6. A Study on the Social Challenges faced by the Queer Community in Chennai

Ms. Maria Jayanthi Jerome, Assistant Professor & Ms. Nisha, II MSW
PG Department of Social Work, Self-Financed Stream,
Madras School of Social Work, Chennai

INTRODUCTION

The queer population in Chennai is visually present as people who are oppressed or discriminated against by the dominant societal structure that has not changed its biased perception of 'queer' from prejudiced cultural and religious beliefs and norms. Queer rights are still intensely argued all over the world: India is no exception; this virtually makes life extremely difficult for identified queer persons, more so in social, economic, and political domains. This is a community that is often discriminated against, violated and rejected that demands further attention. Therefore, this paper aims to review issues of social injustice among queer population in Chennai, how such challenges affect them, and how to find a way forward towards fighting for justice for queer people in Chennai.

The term "queer" serves as an inclusive umbrella for diverse sexual orientations and gender identities, rejecting traditional binaries. LGBTQ+ terminology, including identities like lesbian, gay, bisexual, transgender, intersex, asexual, and pansexual, highlights the community's diversity.

This paper highlights some of the queer issues in society and to grasp the issues mentioned above, it is important to have a basic definition of certain terms including sex, gender and gender identity. Sex means the natural classification based on the difference at the time of birth, while gender means a socially constructed system of roles and duties, which are assigned to male and female, and gender identity is a set of personal experiences that make an individual different from his or her sex. One must distinguish these significations to grasp the profound dynamics of queer selves. Traditional usage of the word "queer", which was a negative label used against homosexual individuals, has been gradually reclaimed as a subversive identity politics. Queer individuals in South Asia have always experienced social isolation and aggressiveness rising from queer hatreds augmented by caste, class, religion, and other factors (Dutta and Roy, 2014). Common barriers include familial rejection, social ostracism, and systemic exclusion from education, healthcare, and employment. Institutional challenges, such as bullying in schools and workplace discrimination, are common. Legal progress, including the decriminalisation of homosexuality and recognition of transgender identities, marks important milestones, but comprehensive anti-discrimination laws are lacking (Math and Seshadri, 2013).

It is important to note that homosexuality and gender non-conformity is not a new phenomenon in India. History recognizes it with Rig Veda and the Kamasutra endorsing same sex relations and gender nonconforming individuals respectively. It was least suppressed during pre-colonial India, then Vedic brahmanic India, does not speak well of homosexuality but it tolerated it more than any other society in the ancient world. Social taboo and legal oppression of homosexuals existed for a long time during which the Queer community was ostracised and persecuted. Legal and cultural repression persisted for centuries until global movements, efforts by NGOs, Pride marches, and government initiatives like the Garima Greh scheme have contributed to reducing stigma, especially for transgender individuals (Rachit Sharma, 2021).

Stereotypical portrayals of queer people have been an issue in the mass media since their integration, however, representations of queer characters in the Indian film industry helped further shift the perspective from the public (Bala and Gupta, 2024). Nevertheless, acceptance is a different phenomenon depending on regional and social criteria, which show that the rural population is much more reluctant. Even though Queer people make up a conservative estimate of 10% of India's population, only less than 2% are comfortable enough to reveal the truth about themselves due to prejudice ingrained into society.

This particular paper calls for continued initiatives to combat queer persons' legal, social and cultural plight in Chennai and more generally in India. Education and equal policies govern the main principles that will lead society toward equal acceptance of people.

Significance of the study

The research aims to provide an in-depth understanding of how social expectations, legal frameworks, and cultural norms impact the daily lives of queer individuals in Chennai. By focusing on core issues such as stigma, discrimination, and exclusion from essential services, this study seeks to amplify the voices of the marginalised queer community. The primary goal is to examine how queer individuals navigate the challenges to maintain their well-being.

This study will contribute to a nuanced understanding of the queer community's lived experiences and will provide empirical data for socially inclusive strategies aimed at fostering acceptance which would be crucial for policymakers, activists, and organisations advocating for Queer rights.

Qualitative data was gathered through interviews with a diverse group of respondents, ensuring that all segments of the queer community, including transwomen, transmen, bisexual, gay, etc, are represented. Ultimately, this research underscores the urgent need for justice, equality, and the protection of the basic rights of queer individuals, who continue to face systemic violations of their freedoms in Chennai and across India.

REVIEW OF LITERATURE

Queer Theory serves as a foundational framework for understanding Queers experiences in the Indian context. As discussed by Dutta and Roy (2014), this theory challenges the rigid binaries of gender and sexuality, advocating for fluid and inclusive understandings of identity. The authors argue that imposing Western frameworks on Indian queer identities overlooks the cultural and historical nuances unique to the region. Intersectionality, a concept developed by Kimberlé Crenshaw, is another critical framework utilised by researchers like Sharma (2021) and Moitra et al. (2020) highlighting how various forms of discrimination based on caste, gender, class, and sexual orientation interact to create unique challenges for individuals. This framework is essential for understanding the diverse struggles within India's queer community and for crafting inclusive policies that address these interconnected forms of marginalisation

Roy and Bajpai (2020) work on lesbian and gay people's negative perceptions and show that cultural resistance is rooted in the organisation. These attitudes are due to the acceptance of heterosexism as the only valid sexual orientation that is encouraged by politics of conservatively constructed family norms, religion and culture. It not only isolates Queer people but they also experience harassment in verbal, physical, or even emotional context all because of their orientation. Likewise, Sharma (2021) appreciates the progressive measures garnered via legal frameworks, for instance the recent liberation of the rights of homosexuals, but the enduring social prejudice in India. Even as criminalisation has been lifted through the judgement in Sec 377, societal prejudices which are deeply entrenched in patriarchal formations continue to exclude queer people from the realm of the viable 'sayable' and thus render them as 'unspeakable.' Singh and Chatterjee (2022) further note that the organisational contexts often echo these social discriminations and Queer workers experience marginalisation and unfair treatment and limited opportunities because organisations do not try enough to be inclusive.

The rights of Queer people were transformed in India in 2018 with the elimination of penalties for homosexuality. However, this is not the end of the legal combat. Currently, marriage of same-sex is not legal, and there is no clear law that offers non discrimination for the gay, lesbian, bisexual and the transgender in matters relating to school, workplace or public places. Sharma (2021) draws us to the fact that despite certain juridical changes for queer people, many still suffer from family rejection or violence from community members and exclusion in these basic needs as housing and employment. According to Singh and Chatterjee (2022), although aspects such as legal changes would be helpful for change, it will not change the prejudicial institutional culture at the ground level without changing the education and community of the institution.

To foster acceptance and inclusion, the authors propose several strategies. Sharma (2021) suggests incorporating comprehensive sex education in schools to challenge stereotypes and promote understanding of diverse identities. Bala and Gupta (2024) argue for more diverse and authentic portrayals of queer lives in media, which can significantly influence public opinion. Singh and Chatterjee (2022) recommend workplace reforms, such as implementing anti-discrimination policies, creating LGBTQ+ support groups, and conducting sensitivity training to ensure inclusivity. Community-led initiatives, such as Pride marches and support networks, also play a vital role in increasing visibility and fostering solidarity among queer individuals. While legal progress has been made, societal acceptance lags behind, with discrimination and marginalisation persisting in various forms. The integration of intersectionality and queer theory into research and advocacy efforts is crucial for addressing these challenges. By focusing on education, media representation, workplace inclusivity, and decolonizing queer identities, a more equitable and inclusive society can be built. These studies underscore the need for sustained efforts to bridge the gap between legal rights and societal acceptance, ensuring dignity, equality, and justice for all queer individuals.

METHODOLOGY

The study follows a qualitative research paradigm to understand the social problems of the queer community in Chennai. The study addresses the experiences of this oppressed community and offers coverage of their hardships. The field of study is Chennai and its design is Narrative Inquiry. This is appropriate for the retelling of narratives and for giving voice to those who are often neglected. Such a method enables the investigator to provide detailed information about the experiences of the studied individuals in a narrative that will also unveil various systems' outer features.

The population for this study is 10 respondents from the queer community in Chennai. In order to access such individuals Snowball Sampling technique was used because the individuals are often a socially stigmatised group or are afraid to reveal their identity. This approach harnesses the confidence within the community leading to enhanced participation. The process of data collection involved in depth interviews as the main tool. They ensured that everyone has their own space and comfort zone to express themselves. These interviews involved asking participants specific broad questions about discrimination, marginalisation or access to resources using the Interview Guide. Also, observation was used to capture data on participants' engagements and behaviours in communal and personal domains, showing the ordinarily invisible social stigma and resilience practices.

Primary and secondary data collection was used in this study. Main data was collected through interviews whereas secondary data from academic literature was used to look at trends and fill literature gaps. This methodology aims to provide a comprehensive exploration of the systemic barriers and discrimination encountered by the queer community. It emphasises inclusivity and sensitivity while striving to highlight the voices and experiences of individuals navigating the margins of Chennai's socio-cultural fabric.

FINDINGS

The queer community in Chennai continues to grapple with systemic social challenges despite recent legal progress in India. While the decriminalisation of Section 377 of the Indian Penal Code in 2018 marked a significant victory for LGBTQ+ rights, societal acceptance remains limited. The challenges encountered by the queer community in Chennai are multifaceted, stemming from cultural conservatism, religious opposition, and institutional neglect. Studies have shown that nearly 80% of LGBTQ+ individuals in India experience discrimination in some form, whether in their families, workplaces, educational institutions, or public spaces.

Stigma

All 10 individuals who were interviewed, mentioned that stigma was one of the basic social challenges they faced till date.

Heterosexuality is the only acceptable norm. This "heteronormative" mindset assumes that everyone naturally identifies as heterosexual and aligns with traditional gender roles. Consequently, individuals who deviate from these norms are often perceived as unnatural, immoral, or deviant. These perceptions manifest in various forms of social exclusion, bullying, and outright hostility toward queer individuals.

Religious Conservatism interprets homosexuality and transgender identities as sinful or against divine will. Such views are often used to justify discriminatory behaviour, alienation, and even violence. These attitudes discourage queer individuals from openly expressing their identities, forcing them to live in secrecy and isolation to avoid ostracism or retaliation from their communities.

Family expectations and honour, where societal norms prioritise marriage, reproduction, and adherence to traditional family structures. Queer individuals often face immense pressure to conform to these norms, with families viewing their identities as a source of shame. Many are subjected to forced marriages or even conversion therapy in a bid to "cure" them of their non-normative sexual orientations or gender identities.

Economic stigma also affects the queer community, especially transgender individuals, who are often seen as unfit for "respectable" jobs. As a result, many are pushed into begging or sex work, reinforcing stereotypes that marginalize them further. This cycle of discrimination and economic exclusion deprives queer individuals of the opportunity to lead fulfilling, dignified lives.

Family Rejection

Based on the conservative culture and expectations that families hold across the world, the queer individual is always seen as rebellious and an outlaw from the ordinary norms set in the community, as well as the nuclear family. Often, rejection from family leads to additional symptoms of the mental health of the person, which includes anxiety and depression, feeling isolated and having low self-esteem. Further, the cost implication of family rejection is high. Eight queer people, especially trans persons and gay are kicked out of their families and are left with no homes and no means of earning a living. Once they've reached this point, they are separated from mainstream society and are unable to receive proper support for their children either financially or emotionally so must turn to other people such as friends or engage in low paid jobs.

Harassment

Transgender women and gay people are particularly at risk of violence and harassment due to prejudice and hatred. Seven out of ten queer individuals confessed that they have faced different kinds of harassment in the society. Transgender women shared that she has been attacked in markets or neighbourhoods leading to physical abuse. Such violence not only harms their health but also fosters fear and discourages them from openly expressing their identities. Verbal abuse, such as name-calling, ridicule, insults, obscene gestures, and threats, was rampant. For instance, gay individuals endure bullying in educational institutions, where they were mocked with derogatory remarks, making the classroom environment hostile.

Sexual violence is another grave issue, with incidents like "corrective rape," where relatives or acquaintances attempt to force queer individuals into heterosexuality. Additionally, queer individuals are often perceived as easy targets, leading to unwanted advances from acquaintances and strangers. Institutional harassment was also prevalent, particularly in police stations, where transgender individuals report being coerced into providing sexual favours to access public utilities. These examples underscore the urgent need for legal protections and awareness campaigns to ensure a safe and inclusive environment for the queer community in Chennai.

Mental Health Issues

All the queer individuals interviewed have faced significant mental health issues like depression, suicidal thoughts, mental torture, and social anxiety, driven by stigma, discrimination, and rejection. Depression is prevalent due to familial exclusion and societal marginalisation, leaving individuals feeling isolated. A young gay man reported battling depression after his family disowned him for coming out. Suicidal thoughts arise when individuals face violence from their own family members, as seen in cases where transwomen were beaten up everyday to push them towards killing oneself, safeguarding honour in the society.

Mental torture was experienced through everyday microaggressions, such as derogatory comments, harassment, or being forced into conversion therapies. A transman was being pressured into a heterosexual marriage despite his protests. Social anxiety stems from fear of judgement in public spaces, leading individuals to avoid social interactions altogether. A gay shared his struggle with panic attacks after repeated instances of harassment on public transport. These mental health issues highlight the urgent need for accessible, queer-affirmative mental health services and societal awareness to alleviate their suffering.

Discrimination in Key Sectors

Queer individuals face significant discrimination across various sectors. In education, bullying, exclusion, and harassment were common, with 6 individuals suffering from mockery and neglect by peers and teachers. For instance, a gay student shared how being ridiculed destroyed his self-esteem and indirectly affected his academic performance. In healthcare, 5 queer individuals had often encountered ridicule or judgement from medical professionals. Transgender individuals, in particular, faced denial of treatment and insensitivity during consultations, discouraging them from seeking necessary medical care. Housing discrimination is another major challenge, as landlords frequently refused to rent to 5 queer individuals due to societal prejudice. For example, a trans couple was evicted after neighbours complained, leaving them vulnerable and without shelter.

In public places like police stations, instead of finding protection, 6 out of 10 queer individuals have often faced harassment and victim-blaming. A transgender sex worker recounted how police officers ridiculed her complaint of assault, demanded favours, and even threatened her with arrest. Discrimination also extends to workplaces, where 4 out of 10 queer individuals faced bias, limited career opportunities, and job insecurity. A transwoman shared her experience of being laid off because her identity was deemed "incompatible" with the work culture. These examples highlight the pervasive discrimination faced by the queer community and underscore the urgent need for systemic change and inclusive policies to address these challenges.

Lack of Institutional Support

Self-realisation for all queer population is a lonely endeavour: There is no social support and very often no positive role model. For instance a young bisexual was saddened that if one can not find friends who understand bisexuality then they start questioning themselves. Furthermore, without information from queer support groups or NGOs people have no direction on how to approach the social, legal and even emotional aspects of their queerness. Especially when this is a problem they have to overcome on their own due to lack of resources from family and society.

RECOMMENDATIONS

Political Level

Legal changes and public awareness crusades should be implemented to enhance the society's acceptance of queer people and their protection. The fair provisions of the anti-discrimination policy in education, employment, health care as well as in the public facilities, including legalization of adoption rights may guarantee equal opportunities for men and women in familial and social contexts. These measures should be coupled with the periodically revived checkups in order to correspond to the needs of the community. At the same time, regardless of the focused media and art campaigns or community programs, people's prejudice can be changed. Better targeted campaigns in schools and universities as well as improvements in existing digital initiatives can help more queer-positive stories be spread and debunk common misconceptions regarding queer people.

Societal Level

Incorporation of an elastic society needs to include education, employment and medical services for everyone. Teachers can include and portray sex and gender education as part of required school curriculum and support it with books and other educating materials with focus on empathy and respect for different people's choices. In the corporate world, measures such as implementing mandatory diversity and sensitivity training, supporting queer employee resource groups, offering grievance procedures and through measures of corporate taxation, offering incentives for companies which engage in the promotion of queer inclusion are necessary steps. In health care, staff sensitivity training for queer health consumer needs, the creation of queer affirmative clinics for physical and mental health, and queer reproductive health programs, consider 24/7 helplines and online consultation services.

Support Networks and Safe Spaces

Strengthening support networks and creating safe spaces are vital for the well-being of queer individuals. Fostering collaborations among NGOs to pool resources and community-based networks can provide safe environments for sharing experiences and seeking guidance, fostering a sense of belonging. Establishing shelter homes for those facing homelessness or violence due to their sexual orientation or gender identity is crucial for offering immediate protection and support. Additionally, resource centers equipped with counseling services, legal aid, and crisis intervention mechanisms can serve as comprehensive hubs for addressing the diverse challenges faced by the queer community.

Police Sensitization

Mandatory training programs should be implemented to prevent harassment and discrimination, fostering understanding and respect within the police force. Establishing dedicated police desks or appointing officers trained to handle LGBTQ+ concerns can provide a supportive and secure avenue for addressing grievances. These measures will help build trust between the queer community and law enforcement, promoting justice and inclusivity.

Individual level

Parent and individual counseling services are essential for fostering acceptance and support within families and empowering queer individuals. Counseling programs for parents and families can help them better understand and embrace their queer members, creating a nurturing and inclusive home environment. Additionally, individual therapy sessions addressing self-esteem, mental health challenges, and coping mechanisms can provide personalized support, helping queer individuals navigate societal pressures and enhance their overall well-being.

By integrating these recommendations into a cohesive strategy, policymakers, organizations, and communities can work together to create a society where queer individuals can thrive without fear of discrimination or exclusion.

CONCLUSION

This study highlights the persistent social barriers faced by queer individuals in Chennai. It underscores the urgent need for structural reforms, cultural shifts, and policy interventions to achieve justice, equality, and dignity for the queer community. By addressing these challenges through education, advocacy, and legal protections, society can move closer to an inclusive and equitable future where every individual, regardless of their sexual orientation or gender identity, can thrive.

REFERENCES

1. Bala, S., & Gupta, T. (2024, July 5). From Taboo to Acceptance: Tracing the Depiction of Indian Queer Sub-Culture in Bollywood.

2. Dutta, A., & Roy, R. (2014). Decolonizing Transgender in India. In TSQ: Transgender Studies Quarterly (p. 320).

3. Issues and Problems Concerning LGBT Persons – Rights of Minorities andotherMarginalisedGroups.(n.d.b).https://ebooks.inflibnet.ac.in/hrdp06 /chapter/issues-and-problems-concerning-lgbt-per sons/

4. Math, S. B., & Seshadri, S. P. (2013). The invisible ones: sexual minorities. The Indian journal of medical research, 137(1), 4–6.

5. Sex and Gender Identity. (n.d.). Planned Parenthood. https://www.plannedparenthood.org/learn/gender-identity/sex-gender-identity

6. Sharma, R. (2021). Rights of LGBTQ in India and the Struggle for Societal Acceptance. In International Journal of Law Management and Humanities (Vol. 4, Issue 3, pp. 18–32). International Journal of Law Management & Humanities.

7. Singh, N., & Chatterjee, A. (2019). Social and Workplace Issues of LGBT Community in India. In The Haryana Police Journal: Vol.2.

8. Thomas, S. S., & Varina, R. (2024, May 14). Unpacking the Term "the Queer," Its History, and WhatItReallyMeans.Cosmopolitan.https://www.cosmopolitan.com/sex-love/a25243218/queer-meaning-definition/

9. User, U. (2023, October 27). What are the main challenges facing the LGBTQ+ community in terms of social justice and how can they be addressed? - Universal Group of Institutions. UniversalGroupofInstitutions.https://universalinstitutions.com/what-are-the-main-challenges-facing-the-lgbtq-community-in-terms-of-social-justice-and-how-can-they-be-addressed/

10. Years after decriminalization of homosexuality, inclusivity is still a dream for the LGBTQ community. (2023, February 14). Times of India Blog.

11.https://timesofindia.indiatimes.com/readersblog/alcoholabuse/years-after-decriminaliz ation-of-homosexuality-inclusivity-is-still-a-dream-for-the-lgbtq-community-50482/

7. Silent Suffering: Leadership Neglect and the Caste Chains of Sanitation Workers in India

Mr. J. P. Francis Dhivakar
Assistant Professor, Department of Social Work, SFS,
Madras Christian College, Chennai

INTRODUCTION

According to the Ministry of Housing and Urban Affairs, Government of India, sanitation workers are those who are hired to maintain sewage systems, clean public areas, remove trash, clean toilets, and guarantee hygienic conditions in both urban and rural regions. Around the world, the late 18th century saw the industrial revolution, which resulted in numerous important changes to laws, technology, and other areas. The emergence of labour movements is one consequence of the industrial revolution. Workers were subjected to long hours, unfavourable working conditions, low pay, and hazardous workplaces as industries started to replace humans with robots. Workers were prompted to defend their rights by these circumstances. Numerous beneficial improvements were introduced with the establishment of labour unions, including the implementation of 8-hour workdays, a checkpoint on worker exploitation, the guarantee of minimum salaries, and more. However, the rights and difficulties faced by manual scavengers and sanitary workers are not as well-known as those of other workers. Particularly in India, their problems and difficulties are either disregarded or not given enough attention. This article explores the life of sanitation workers through literature, the caste chain of sanitation workers & the perceptions of leaders of past and present on sanitation workers.

Tracing back the life of Sanitation Workers and Manual Scavengers through Novels

Sundara Ramasamy's work Thottiyin Magan, originally written by Thagazhi Sivasankaran Pillai, describes the existence of manual scavengers in the state of Kerala in the 1900s. I want to highlight a few noteworthy incidents from this book that are highly pertinent to the conversation. The narrative first depicts the living conditions and housing communities of manual scavengers. Traditionally, in the caste based society, Manual scavengers are made to live in the outskirts of the village, in the small, unhygienic huts. Mostly the settlements are located near to dumbing yards. Imayam, a Tamil novelist, used rainwater as a metaphor to depict the village's land division in his book Kooveru Kaluthai (The Untethered Donkey) in order to provide a vivid picture of this. The village is structured in a way that the upper-caste households are located at the higher points of the land, where they are untouched by the pollution of the lower caste settlements. These higher areas have clean, unspoiled surroundings, mirroring the social status and privilege enjoyed by the upper castes. In contrast, the Dalit settlements are situated in the low-lying areas of the village. These areas are prone to being flooded when the rains come, symbolizing the social drowning and suffocation of the lower castes under the weight of discrimination and oppression. When the rain falls on the village, it flows from the higher caste areas first, carrying with it dirt, waste, and impurity from the elevated lands. As the water flows downhill, it pollutes the Dalit areas, washing over them and further reinforcing the idea of caste purity and contamination. This water, which should ideally be life-giving, becomes a symbol of how the upper-caste society taints and marginalizes the lower castes. This rigid structure still remained unchanged. Even now, in the village or in urban areas, sanitary workers and manual scavengers are living on the outskirts or in the poor hygienic places. Mostly those places are termed as ‘Colonies’.

In the Thottiyin Magan novel, the author describes the two pandemic diseases called Cholera and Small box which played major roles in the novel. These diseases, exacerbated by poor living conditions and systemic neglect, claim numerous lives. Cholera spreads rapidly due to unsanitary environments, while smallpox thrives amidst lack of medical care and ignorance. The pandemics in the novel underscore the intersection of caste oppression and health disparities, symbolizing how marginalized communities bear the brunt of societal indifference. The society and administrators and bureaucrats are very much indifference towards the health and life of sanitary workers. Their health and life issues never shattered the public and administration consciousness.

The average life expectancy of Sanitary workers is comparatively low. According to a survey by India Development Review (2021), sanitary workers' life expectancy is 40-45 years which is comparatively lower than the national average of 70 years. The work-related mortality is quite high among sanitary workers. According to the report presented by the Union Minister for Social Justice and Empowerment in one of parliament sessions in December 2023, more than 400 people died while cleaning septic tanks and sewers between 2018 and 2023. Tamil Nadu secures 4th position followed by Rajasthan, Gujarat and Maharashtra in terms of high number of registered sewer deaths.

These recent data indicates that the life experience of sanitary workers has not changed significantly in 100 years. They are leading a miserable life even today. Besides the unsafe working conditions and poor standard of living, they are facing caste discrimination as well.

Caste & Sanitation Workers and Manual Scavengers

In India, a person's caste historically determines what they can do for a living. Based on the Varna system, the Indian caste system separates people into four groups: Brahmins, Kshatriyas, Vaishyas, and Sudras. The Kshatriyas are supposed to be administrators and warriors, while the Brahmins are supposed to be instructors and priests. The Sudras are intended to labour in agriculture and be governed by Brahmins, Kshatriyas, and Vaishyas, while the Vaishyas are expected to work as merchants and in commerce. According to the hierarchy, Brahmins have the greatest influence over others, while Sudras are at the bottom, meaning that everyone else is submissive to them. Aside from these categories, there are some individuals who are not considered to be part of the varna system and are referred to as Avarnas. The Avarna people are regarded as the lowest class in society, with their sole responsibility being to obey and work for the Varna people. They are expected to perform menial and inhumane tasks such as cleaning human excreta, cleaning dead animals, washing, and other menial activities. The caste system allows for untouchability at varying levels. Dr. Ambedkar describes the Indian caste structure as 'Graded Inequality'. People practiced and experienced untouchability at varying levels. The Avarna people are the most vulnerable, having endured a variety of discriminations and untouchability practices in society. Nowadays, the Avarna people are referred to as Dalits in India. In India, Dalits are expected to perform sanitary duties. According to the Varna system, they are responsible for both sanitary and manual scavenging.

Following independence and the establishment of the Indian Constitution, the caste structure was fractured and made more flexible. All types of untouchability are outlawed by Article 17 of the Indian Constitution. Article 46 requires the State to safeguard the weaker segments of society, especially the Scheduled Castes and Tribes, from social injustice and all types of exploitation, and to advance their economic and educational interests with particular attention. As a result, several changes have been made to the caste system, one of which is the ability for people to pick their own occupations. Nonetheless, sanitation workers and manual scavengers do not receive this relaxation or luxury on a social level. Dalits continue to perform these tasks. Still society expects traditionally Dalit people to do these inhumane works. Even among the Dalits, only very few castes are forced to do these inhumane works. Here are some historical caste names that have been associated with sanitation work in different states of India:

Valmiki or Balmiki (also referred to as Mehtar, Dom, Chuhra, or Chamar) - Uttar Pradesh, Madhya Pradesh, Rajasthan, Bihar, Jharkhand, Punjab, Haryana, and other parts of North India.

Hela (also referred to as Halalkhor) - West Bengal, Odisha, Assam, and other parts of East India.

Arunthathiyar or Chakkiliyar - Tamil Nadu.

Madiga or Mala - Andhra Pradesh and Telangana.

Adi Dravidar or Paraiyar - Tamil Nadu and Kerala.

According to the very recent report by the Union Government (2024), as part of profiling sewer and septic tank workers under NAMASTE program was brought as replacement of existing scheme of the Self Employment Scheme for Rehabilitation of Manual Scavengers (SRMS), it is found that of the profiled 38000 workers from 3000 local bodies in 29 states and Union territories, 77.2% of them belong to SC/ST category (The Hindu, 29.09.2024). This report itself is obvious evidence that sanitary related works are predominantly done by the people from SC and ST categories.

Perspectives of Leaders- Gandhi & Ambedkar, Current Leaders

When we are looking for solutions for sanitary workers' issues, we ought to examine the attitudes of leaders in the past and present towards sanitary workers. The argument between Dr. Ambedkar and Mahatma Gandhi's points of view on Sanitary workers and Manual scavengers is presented in Arundhati Roy's book, "The Doctor and the Saint." As the Father of our Nation, Mahatma Gandhi regarded and referred to the Dalits as "Harijans," which translates to "children of God." He extolled sanitation workers' labours. He declared that sanitary personnel are doing an excellent job of cleaning the entire society, and as a result, the society is hygienic and clean. By performing housekeeping duties, they are directly honouring the gods. Their efforts ought to be honoured and recognised. They are fortunate to be doing this task. I would also perform their work if I had the chance.

On the contrary to this view, Dr. Ambedkar, who rose from an untouchable community, stated that sanitary workers should withdraw their works. They should realize that what they are doing is not a holy job rather it is inhumane and mean jobs. They should realize that they are enslaved into this job because of their birth, not by their willingness. They should liberate themselves from these inhumane occupations. These views give us an understanding of two extreme perspectives of people about sanitary workers and manual scavengers.

Investigating the attitudes of current state and federal officials towards sanitary workers reveals that they in some way mirror and uphold

Mahatma Gandhi's views. The honourable prime minister used to extol and commend sanitation personnel for their efforts. The honourable Prime Minister Narendra Modi honoured five sanitary workers by washing their feet during the 2019 Kumbh Mela celebration in Prayagraj, then in Allahabad. In the meeting, he said that interacting with sanitary workers is the most treasured moment and experience for him which he won't forget in his lifetime. He also referred to sanitary workers as "Karmayogis" during the address (Times of India, 25.02.2019). A month ago, the honourable Chief Minister of Tamil Nadu had a dine in with sanitary workers as a token of appreciation of their works during the heavy rainfall in Chennai (Time of India, 17.10.2024). These two instances and statements somewhat support Mahatma Gandhi's viewpoint of the exaltation of sanitation workers, which rarely results in practical remedies for their problems in the social, economic, and professional spheres. because these leaders' motions and expressions are in contrast to the genuine demands of sanitation workers.

The demands of Sanitation Workers

The next day of Prime Minister Modi's action at Prayagraj, a collective of Sanitation workers called Aadi Dharm Samaaj staged a protest in Delhi along with hundreds of sanitary workers demanding tangible measures to cease man-handling practices of human excreta and better lives of sanitation workers. During the demonstration, the organizer of the group questioned what is the use of washing feet when the government has not taken action to prevent those bare feet from getting into drainage (The Hindu, 25.02.2019). As correctly noted, as of right now, no one has been found guilty under The Prohibition of Employment as Manual Scavengers and Their Rehabilitation Act, 2013, which forbids hiring anyone to perform hazardous cleaning of septic tanks and sewers or to build or maintain unhygienic restrooms.

Similarly, in the last couple of years, Tamil Nadu witnessed a handful of protests of sanitary workers demanding decent wage and wage hike, permanency of work, decent work life. For instance, on 22nd October 2024, sanitation workers staged a protest demanding better daily wages in Tuticorin (The Hindu, 22.10.2024). At the state level conference hosted by the Madurai Legal Awareness Coordination Committee (MLACC) in Virudhunagar on June 22, 2024, sanitation workers from several village panchayats in Virudhunagar and Madurai came together to express their demands for increased compensation, clear work schedules, and an end to caste discrimination.

CONCLUSION

This article tried to explore the lives and demands of sanitation workers and manual scavengers in India through novels and leaders' approach. As mentioned earlier, this unfocused and less spoken working class should be given more attention and intervention. The intervention at the macro level among the all citizens of this country has to be given in order to break their own caste consciousness related to the occupation. The caste consciousness and prejudice mindset of common people are the biggest hindrances to break the caste chains and leadership neglect of sanitation workers. The Gandhian approach will only help the society to maintain this unfair hierarchical occupation structure. Whereas the Ambedkarite approach will end this inhumane and unfair hierarchical structure. Addressing the real issues alone will bring positive progressive changes in the life of sanitation workers, not mere glorification and distributing placebo.

REFERENCES

1. Arundhati Roy (2017), The Doctor and The Saint, Penguin Random House India Publication.

2. Imayam (1994), Koveru Kaluthaikal, Narmadha Publication.

3. Sundara Ramasamy (1997) originally by Thagazhi Sivasankaran Pillai (1947), Thottiyin Magan Novel, Kalachuvadu Publication.

4. Business Standard (2023), Over 400 died while cleaning septic tanks, sewers in India between 2018-23, www.business-standard.com, 05.12.2023.

5. India Development Review (2021), Published in Times of India dated 22.08.2021.

6. The Hindu (2019), Sanitation workers slam Modi govt, www.thehindu.com, 25.02.2019.

7. The Hindu, (2023), Poverty, Caste – Discrimination at the root of manual scavenging, Reveals study, www.thehindu.com, 07.01.2023.

8. The Hindu (2024), 92% of workers cleaning urban sewers, septic tanks are from SC, ST, OBC groups, www.thehindu.com, 29.09.2024.

9. The Hindu (2024), Sanitary workers stage protest demanding better wages, www.thehindu.com, 22.10.2024.

10. The New Indian Express, 2023, Only SCs as sanitary workers in TN's Tirupur, www.newindianexpress.com, 18.04.2023.

11. The Times of India (2019), PM Narendra Modi washes feet of sanitary workers, www.timesofindia.com, 25.09.2019.

12. The Times of India (2021), No progress for sanitation workers: What must change, www.timesofindia.com, 22.08.2021.

13. The Times of India (2024), Sanitation workers demand better pay, well-defined work timings, www.timesofindia.com, 23.06.2024.

14. The Times of India (2024), Stalin dines with sanitary staffers who worked during Chennai rain, www.timesofindia.com, 17.10.2024.

15. The Wire, 2021, Here's what needs to change for sanitation works in India, www.thewire.in, 22.08.2021.

8. புறந்தள்ளலைப் புறந்தள்ளும் புறநானூற்றுப் பாடல்கள்

முனைவர் த. செபுலோன் பிரபு துரை
உதவிப் பேராசிரியர், தமிழ்த்துறை,
சென்னைக் கிறித்தவக் கல்லூரி

மாந்தரினம் அற வழியில் செல்வதற்காக உலகில் பல அமைப்புகள், சமயங்கள் கருத்துக்களை வழங்கியுள்ளன. அவ்வகையில் எந்த சமயமும் சாராமல் எந்த கடவுளையும் முதன்மையாக்காமல் மக்கள் இனத்துக்கு மக்களே அறவுரை கூறும் அல்லது மக்கள் வாழ்வியலை மாண்புகளை பதிவு செய்யும் நூலாக புறநானூறு விளங்குகிறது. புறநானூறு பல்வேறு காலகட்டங்களில் பல்வேறு பாவலர்களால் பல்வேறு இடங்களில் பல்வேறு மைய கருத்துக்களை வைத்து பாடப்பெற்ற நூல்களின் தொகுதி என்பது நாம் அறிந்தது. இப்புறநானூற்றுப் பாடல்களில் மாந்தர் இனத்தின் விழுமியமாக யாரும் யாருக்கும் அடிமை இல்லை. எல்லோரும் இணையானவர்கள் என்ற கருத்தை வலியுறுத்தும் பாடல்கள் சிலவற்றை மட்டும் பின்வருமாறு காணலாம்

புறநானூறு

புறநானூறு சங்க இலக்கியங்களுள் எட்டுத்தொகை நூல்களில் குறிப்பிட தகுந்த நூலாகும். இப்பாடல்களில் வெட்சி, கரந்தை, வஞ்சி, காஞ்சி, நொச்சி, உழிஞை, தும்பை, வாகை, பாடாண், பொதுவியல், கைக்கிளை, பெருந்திணை ஆகிய புறத்திணைகளும் அவற்றின் துறைகளும் பயின்றுவருகின்றன. இது, பண்டைக்காலத்தில் தமிழ்நாட்டை ஆண்ட மூவேந்தர்கள், சிற்றரசர்கள், வேளிர்கள், கடையெழு வள்ளல்கள், புலவர்கள், மக்கள் வாழ்க்கை முறை, உணவு, உடை, விழாக்கள் முதலிய பல செய்திகளைப் புலப்படுத்தும் வரலாற்றுப் பெருநூலாகவும் தமிழர்களின் செந்நெறிப் பெட்டகமாகவும் திகழ்கிறது. இப்பாடல்கள் பல மையப் பொருட்களைக் கொண்டு பாடப் பெற்றிருந்தாலும் யாரும் யாருக்கும் இழிஞர் இல்லை அனைவரும் இணையானவர்கள் என்னும் கருத்தை முன்வைக்கின்றன. மக்களின வாழ்க்கை என்பது எந்த ஏற்றத்தாழ்வுகளும் இல்லாமல் எல்லோரையும் நேசிக்கிற

ஒன்றாக பார்க்கிற ஒரு அமைப்பாக இருந்தால் தான் பொது தன்மை வாய்ந்ததாக இருக்கும் என்பதை எந்த மதப் பின்னணியும் கடவுள் பின்னணியும் கொள்ளாமல் இயற்றப்பட்ட பாடல்களாக புறநானூற்று பாடல்கள் அமைகின்றன

உயர்வுத்தாழ்வும் தமிழர் மரபும்

மாந்தர்களை உயர்வாகவும் பிற உயிர்களை சற்று தாழ்வாகவும் பார்க்கிற அல்லது நடத்துகிற சூழல் உலகமெங்கும் உள்ளன குறிப்பாக ஒரு நாடு என்பது அடிமைகள் இல்லாமல் இருப்பது எந்த வகையிலும் அறம் அல்ல முதலிய கருத்துக்கள் சில பண்பாட்டின் அடிப்படை கருத்துகளாகவே இருந்துள்ளதை வரலாறு நமக்கு உணர்த்துகிறது. தமிழர் மாந்தர்களை மட்டுமல்லாது பிற உயிர்களையும் நேசித்ததோடு மாண்பளித்தும் வந்தனர். அவைகளுக்கு பெயர் வைத்ததிலிருந்தும் அவைகளை அழைத்ததிலிருந்தும் பண்பாட்டின் மாண்பை அறிய முடிகிறது. குறிப்பாக தமிழரின் இலக்கண நூலாகிய தொல்காப்பியம் மாந்தர் இனத்தை உயர்திணை என்றும் மாந்தர் அல்லாத பிற உயிர்களை அஃறிணை என்றும் குறித்து இருக்கிறது. உயர்திணைக்கு எதிர்ச்சொல் தாழ்த்திணை அல்லது கீழ்திணை என்றுதான் குறிப்பிடபெற வேண்டும். ஆனால் தொல்காப்பியம் அவ்வாறு குறிப்பிடாமல் அஃறிணை என்று குறித்து இருக்கிறது. உயர்வு அல்லாத திணை என்பது அதன் பொருள். உயர்வுக்கு எதிர் தாழ் அல்லது கீழ் ஆனால் உயர்வு அல்லாதது என்று கூறுவது அடிப்படை பண்பாடு எனத் துணியலாம். மாந்தரினத்தின் காதல் உணர்வைப் பதிவு செய்யும் வகையில் இயற்றப்பெற்ற பகுதியில்

எல்லா உயிர்க்கும் இன்பம் என்பது

தானமர்ந்து வரூஉம் மேவற் றாகும் (பொருளியல்1168)

மாந்தரினத்திற்கு மட்டமல்ல காதல் என்னும் உணர்வு உலகில் உள்ள அனைத்து உயர்களுக்கும் பொதுவானது. என்ற கருத்தை முன்வைக்கிறது தொல்காப்பியம். மேலும் ஒரு காயின் சுவை கசப்புத் தன்மை கொண்டதாக இருக்கும் பொழுது கசப்பு காய் என்று அதற்கு பெயரிடாமல் இனிப்பு அற்ற காய் என்று அழைத்திருக்கின்றனர். பாகற்காய்க்கு கசப்புகாய் என பெயர்

வைக்காமல் பாகு + அல் +காய் என்று வைத்தமை நோக்கத்தக்கது.

தமிழரின் இலக்கண நூலும் மக்கள் பெயர்வைத்தமையும் இவ்வாறு இருக்க, தமிழின் அடையாளமாக திகழும் திருக்குறள் மாந்தரினத்தின் அறிவை எத்தகைய அளவுகோலால் எவ்வாறு கணக்கிடலாம் என்று வெளிப்படுத்த

அறிவினான் ஆகுவ துண்டோ பிறிதின்நோய்

தந்நோய்போல் போற்றாக் கடை. - 315

இடம் பெறுகிறது. பிறரின் நோய் என்று எழுதி இருந்தால் அக்குறள் மிக இயல்பான ஒரு பொருளைக் கொண்டதாக இருந்திருக்கும். ஆனால் பிறிதின்நோய் என்று குறிப்பிட்டதினால் பிறரின் நோயை எவ்வாறு உணர்ந்து கொள்கிறோமோ அதைப்போலவே பிரிதின் நோயையும் அதாவது, அஃறினை ஒன்றன் பாலையும் வள்ளுவர் குறித்து இருக்கிறார் என்பதை காண முடிகிறது. இவ்வகையில் தமிழ் மொழியின் இலக்கண நூலாகிய தொல்காப்பியத்தில் இருந்து ஒரு சான்றையும் தமிழர் மறை என்று சொல்லப்படுகிற திருக்குறளில் இருந்து ஒரு குறளையும் சான்றாக பார்த்தோம். இவை மாந்தரினத்துக்கு வழிகாட்டிய மறை நூல்களாகவும் நெறி நூல்களாகவும் அமைந்திருப்பதைக் காண முடிகிறது. இவ்வகையில் புறநானூறுப் பாடல்கள் அதிகாரத்தை, அடிமைத்தனத்தை, ஏற்றத்தாழ்வுகளை எதிர்க்கும் கருத்துகளை நேரடியாகவும் மறைமுகமாகவும் சுட்டப்பெற்றிருப்பதைக் காணலாம்.

போரும் புறந்தள்ளலும்

எச்சமுகத்துக்கும் போர் என்பது மிகக் கொடியது. அது மக்களை நேசிக்காமல் கொல்லும், துன்புறுத்தும் செயல்களுக்கு முன்னுரிமை தருவது. எனவே போர் ஒழிக்கப்பட வேண்டும். போர் இன்னொரு நாட்டு மக்களை வெறுப்பதற்கு புறம் தள்ளுவதற்கு அடிப்படையாக அமைகிறது. எனவே போர் நமக்கு பொருத்தம் இல்லாத ஒன்று என்பதை வலியுறுத்தும் நோக்கில் ஓங்கூர் மாசாத்தியார் எழுதிய பாடல் இயற்றப்பெற்றுள்ளது.

கெடுக சிந்தை; கடிது இவள் துணிவே;

மூதில் மகளிர் ஆதல் தகுமே: (ஒக்கூர் மாசாத்தியார் 297)

ஆனால் இப்பாடலைத் தமிழ் சமூகத்தில் இதுவரை எந்தக் கருத்துக்காக இயற்றப்பட்டதோ அந்தக் கருத்தை வலியுறுத்தாமல் அதற்கு மாறான கருத்தையே மக்களிடம் பரப்பி இருக்கிறார்கள் எனலாம். அப்பாடல் கெடுக சிந்தை என்று தொடங்குகிறது. ஒரு பெண் தன் வீட்டில் உள்ள ஆண்களை எல்லாம் போருக்கு அனுப்பி இருக்கிறாள். போருக்குச் சென்றவர்கள் போர்களத்திலே புண்பட்டு வீரச்சாவடைந்து விட்டனர். இந்த நாளும் முரசு சத்தம் கேட்கிறது எனவே விளையாடிக் கொண்டிருந்த தனது ஒரே குழந்தையை அழைத்து, தலைக்கு எண்ணெய் பூசி, மயிரை வாரி முடிந்து, கையிலே வேலைக் கொடுத்து போர்க்களத்துக்கு அனுப்புகிறாள் என்று சொல்லுகின்றது. இந்தப் பாடலின் முதல் அடி இவளுடைய எண்ணம் கெட்டுப் போகட்டும் என்று தொடங்குகிறது. ஆனால் தமிழர்கள் வீரர்கள், மறவர்கள் போரை விரும்புகிறவர்கள் என்றெல்லாம் இதுகாரும் சொல்லப்பட்டு வந்தது. இதையே மக்களும் நம்பினர். நம்பியும் வருகின்றனர். ஆனால் இப்பாடல் போரைப் புறந்தள்ளுகிற, போர் செய்ய வேண்டும் என்கிற எண்ணம் கெட வேண்டும் என்று முன்னிறுத்துகிற பாடலாக இருக்கிறது.

ஆளுமையும் புறந்தள்ளலும்

கணியன் பூங்குன்றனாரின் யாதும் ஊரே யாவரும் கேளிர் என்பது உலகப் புகழ் பெற்ற பாடலாக அறியப்படுகிறது. இந்த உலகம் எனது சிற்றூர். இந்த உலகில் உள்ள அனைத்து மக்களும் எனது உறவினர்கள் என்னும் வலிய கருத்தை முன்வைக்கிறது. அது மட்டுமல்லாமல் இந்த உலகில் மகிழ்ச்சியும் துன்பமும் நிரந்தரமானவைகள் அல்ல, அப்படியே பிறப்பும், இறப்பும். இவ்வுலகில் பிறந்தவர்கள் அனைவரும் இறந்து தான் ஆக வேண்டும் எனவே இவ்வாழ்க்கையை மிக நன்றாகவும் சிறப்பாகவும் வாழ வேண்டும் எனும் கருத்தை முன்வைப்பதோடு வேறு எந்த இனக் குழுவிலும் சொல்லப்பட முடியாத ஒரு செய்தியை இப்பாடல் வைக்கிறது.

யாதும் ஊரே யாவரும் கேளிர்

தீதும் நன்றும் பிறர்தர வாரா

காட்சியில் தெளிந்தனம் ஆகலின், மாட்சியின்

பெரியோரை வியத்தலும் இலமே,

சிறியோரை இகழ்தல் அதனினும் இலமே. (கணியன் பூங்குன்றனார் (192)

அடிகள் இப்பாடலின் தனித்தன்மையை சிறப்புறச் செய்கிறது. மாட்சியில் சிறந்தவர்களை வியப்பதும், மகிழ்வதும், பாராட்டுவதும், போற்றுவதும், வணங்குவதும், புகழ் பாடுவதும் உலக இயற்கையாக அமைகிறது. ஆனால் இப்பாடல் மாட்சியில் பெரியோரை வியத்தலும் இலமே அதைவிட எந்த சிறப்பும் இல்லாதவர்கள் என்று இந்த சமூகத்தால் அடையாளப்படுத்தப்படுகிறவர்களை நாங்கள் இழிவாக பார்ப்பதில்லை. ஏனென்றால் அனைவரும் சமம் என்கிற கருத்தை முன்வைக்கிறது. ஆளுமை மிக்கவர்களை உயர்த்துவதையும் ஆளுமையற்றவர்களை புறம் தள்ளக் கூடாது என்கிற செய்தியையும் இப்பாடல் மூலம் நாம் அறிய முடிகிறது.

தீமை அகற்றலும் புறந்தள்ளலும்

பல் சான்றீரே பல் சான்றீரே எனத் தொடங்கும் பாடல் அகவை முதிர்ந்த காலத்தில் எந்த பயனும் இல்லாமல் இருக்கின்ற பெரியவர்களே உங்களால் நன்மை செய்ய முடியவில்லை என்றாலும் தாழ்வில்லை தீமை செய்யாதிருங்கள். அதுதான் நல்லவர்கள் செல்லுகிற வழி மக்கள் அனைவரும் மகிழ்கிற வழி என்று வலியுறுத்துகிறது. உங்களால் நன்மை செய்ய முடியவில்லை என்றால் தாழ்வில்லை பிறருக்கு தீமை செய்யாமல் இருங்கள்.

நல்லது செய்தல் ஆற்றீர் ஆயினும்

அல்லது செய்தல் ஓம்பு மின்! அதுதான்

எல்லாரும் உவப்பது: அன்றியும்

நல்ஆற்றுப் படூஉம் நெறியுமார் அதுவே! நரிவெரூஉத் தலையார் (195)

இந்த உலக வாழ்வில் பன்னெடுங்காலம் வாழ்ந்து சாவை நெருங்கிக் கொண்டிருக்கிற மக்களுக்கு சொல்லுகிற அறிவுரையாக இருக்கிறது. ஏனென்றால் பெரியவர்கள் சில நேரங்களில் தவறான கருத்துக்களை மக்களினத்திற்கு விட்டுச் செல்வார்கள் அத்தகைய கருத்துக்கள் ஒருவரை புறந்தள்ள கூடாது அனைவரையும் சமமாக நேசிக்க வேண்டும் என்பதை வலியுறுத்துவதாக இந்தப் பாடல் அமைந்திருப்பதை காணலாம்

ஜாதியும் புறந்தள்ளலும்

மாங்குடி கிழாரின் பாடல் புறநானூற்றுப் பாடல்களிலேயே ஒரு தனித்தன்மை வாய்ந்த பாடலாக காணப்படுகிறது. இந்த நிலத்தில் இருக்கின்ற இந்த நிலத்துக்கு உரிமையானவைகளாக சிலவற்றை அடையாளம் காட்டுகின்றது. மலர்கள், உணவு, குடி என்று சில பெயர்களை முன்வைக்கின்றது.

துடியன் பாணன் பறையன் கடம்பனென்று

இந்நான் கல்லது குடியும் இல்லை;

ஒன்னாத் தெவ்வர் முன்னின்று விலங்கி

ஒளிறுஏந்து மருப்பின் களிறுஎறிந்து வீழ்ந்தெனக்

கல்லே பரவின் அல்லது

நெல்உகுத்துப் பரவும் கடவுளும் இலவே மாங்குடி கிழார் (335)

தமிழர் மரபில் குறிஞ்சி, முல்லை, மருதம், நெய்தல், முதலிய மலர்களுக்காக முதன்மைப்படுத்தப்பெற்றவை. அப்படியே குடிகளில் மறையோர் நாட்டின் செய்திகளை சில தமிழ் இலக்கிய இலக்கணங்களும் மேற்கோளாக காட்டி இருக்கின்றன. ஆனால் இப்பாடல் பறையன், துடியன், அல்லாத குடியும் இல்லை என்று வலியுறுத்துகிறது. இத்தகைய வலியுறுத்தல் முதன்மை பெறுவதற்கு அடிப்படையாக இந்த மண்ணில் மக்களுக்காக வாழ்ந்து போரில் வீர சாவடைந்த நடு கல்லே எங்களுக்கு போதுமானது நீங்கள் கொண்டுவரும் கடவுள்கள் எங்களுக்கு தேவையில்லை என்னும் கருத்தே முதன்மையாகிறது. பொருளைக் கொண்டிருக்கிற பாடல் இதுவரை புறந்தள்ளப்பட்ட அல்லது கண்டு கொள்ளப்படாத குடிகளையும் மலர்களையும்

உணவையும் முதன்மைப்படுத்தி பேசுகிறது. விளிம்பு நிலையில் உள்ளவைகளை மையத்துக்கு கொண்டு வருகிற முயற்சியாக இப்பாடலைக் காணலாம்.

பெருவாழ்வும் புறந்தள்ளலும்

நம்பி நெடுஞ்செழியனின் பாடல் மன்னனின் இறப்புக்கு பின்னர் பிள்ளைகள் அல்லது மன்னனைச் சார்ந்தவர்கள் மன்னரின் நண்பர் புலவரிடம் ஏதேனும் கடைசியாக விருப்பத்தைத் தெரிவித்தாரா? புதைக்கச் சொன்னாரா? எரிக்கச் சொன்னாரா? என்பதைப் போல வினவியிருக்கக்கூடும். அதற்கு அவர் விடை சொல்வதாக பாடல் அமைகிறது.

மயக்குடைய மொழிவிடுத்தனன், ஆங்குச்

செய்ப வெல்லாஞ் செய்தன னாகலின்

இடுக வொன்றோ சுடுக வொன்றோ

படுவழிப் படுகவிப் புகழ்வெய்யோன் றலையே நம்பி நெடுஞ்செழியன் (235)

பிறப்பிலிருந்து இறப்பு வரை சடங்குகளும் முறைமைகளும் உயர்வுத் தாழ்வை கற்பிக்கின்றன. இறந்தவர்களுக்கு நல்ல முறையில் மாண்பு அளித்து அவர் உடல்களை அடக்கம் செய்ய வேண்டும் என்பது உலகின் பெரும்பான்மையான நாகரீகம் கொண்ட பண்பாட்டு இன குழுக்களின் அடிப்படை கூறாக பார்க்க முடிகிறது. அவை எகிப்து, சீனம், சுமேரியா, முதலிய நாகரிகத்தைக் கொண்டு இருக்கிற நாடுகளிலும் பழந்தமிழரின் களங்கள் ஆகிய சிந்துவெளி முதல் தமிழ்நாட்டில் இப்போது கிடைக்கப்பெறுகின்ற முதுமக்கள் தாழிகள், பேழைகள் வரையிலான செய்திகள் அவற்றை நமக்கு வலியுறுத்துகின்றன. அத்தகைய சூழலில் ஒரு அரசனுடைய உடலை எவ்வாறு அடக்கம் செய்யலாம் என்று அரசரின் நெருக்கமான நண்பரிடம் வினவிய போது. அவன் தான் செய்ய வேண்டிய வேலைகள் எல்லாம் அவன் சிறப்பாக செய்து முடித்து விட்டான். அவன் செய்வதற்கு என்று பெரிதாக ஒன்றும் இல்லை. அவன் செய்த செயல்கள் அவனுக்கு அடையாளமாகவும் சிறப்பாகவும் திகழ்கின்றன. எனவே உங்கள் விருப்பத்தின்படி அவன் உடலை

புதைக்க வேண்டும் என்றால் புதையுங்கள். எரிக்க வேண்டுமென்றால் எரியுங்கள் என்று சொல்வதாக அமைகிறது. சடங்கையும் முறைமைகளையும் பின்பற்றிக் கொண்டிருக்கிறவர்கள் மக்களுக்கு சமத்துவத்திற்கு முதன்மையளிக்க மாட்டர்கள். இப்பாடல் சடங்கு முறைமைகளுக்கு முதன்மைத் தராமல் மக்கள் நலனையும் சான்றாக வாழ்ந்த சான்றோனுடைய வாழ்க்கையையும் முன்வைக்கிறது.

இத்தகைய தனித்துவமான வாழ்வியல் முறையைப் பின்பற்றியவரே, "இட்டோர் பெரியோர், இடாதோர் இழிகுலத்தோர்" என்றும் "குலதாழ்ச்சி உயர்ச்சி சொல்லல் பாவம்", என்று பதிவு செய்கின்றனர். மொழி, இனம், பால், நாடு, இனம், நிறம், கண்டம் என எத்தகைய பிரிவுகள் இருந்தாலும் யாரும் யாருக்கும் இழிஞர் இல்லை அனைவரும் இணையானவர்கள். மேற்கண்ட பெயர்களில் ஒருவரையும் பிரித்தல் புறந்தள்ளல் நிகழக்கூடாது என்பது தமிழ்ச்சான்றோரின் வாழ்வாகவும் வழியாகவும் இருந்துள்ளதை புறநானூற்றுப் பாடல்கள் உறுதி செய்கின்றன. மாந்தரை மாந்தராக நேசிக்க வேண்டும் பிற உயிர்களையும் பாதுகாக்க வேண்டும் என்பது புறநானூற்று பாடல் வழியில் நாம் அறிய வேண்டும் செய்தியாகும்.

துணைநூல் பட்டியல்

1.புறநானூறு, டாக்டர் உ. வே. சாமிநாதையர் உரையாசிரியர், டாக்டர் உ. வே. சாமிநாதையர் நூல்நிலையம் 2017.

2.உலகம் போற்றும் திருக்குறள் குறளும் பொருளும், லியோ புக் பப்லீஷர்ஸ், 2023

3.அகப்பொருள் கோட்பாடு: தொல்காப்பியம் - சங்க இலக்கியம் ஒப்பீடு, சிலம்பு நா. செல்வராசு, நியு செஞ்சுரி புக் ஹவுஸ், 2018

4.சங்க இலக்கியம் (22 தொகுதிகள்), நியு செஞ்சுரி புக் ஹவுஸ், 2024

5.தமிழ் இலக்கிய வரலாறு, டாக்டர் சி..பாலசுப்பரமணியன், மணமலர்ப் பதிப்பகம்,1998.

9. A Study on the Challenges faced by Transgenders

Ms. Minulin Beaulah A, Ms. Raghu Nandhini K, Mr. Samuel Surendran J, II MSW HRM &

Dr. Baily Vincent, Associate Professor, Department of Social Work, Self-Financed Stream, Madras Christian College, Chennai

INTRODUCTION

The term 'transgender' is commonly used as a broad classification for individuals whose gender identity, expression, or behaviour differs from the sex assigned to them at birth. Generally, transgender individuals can be categorized into two groups. The first group identifies as a third gender, distinct from male or female, and may or may not undergo procedures to remove gender-specific organs. The second group consists of individuals who identify with a gender different from their birth-assigned sex. A few in this group may choose to undergo Sex Reassignment Surgery (SRS), which is not obligatory. This group has sought legal recognition as either male or female according to their personal identity, a right that has been provisionally granted but still faces challenges in practical enforcement. The 2011 Indian census recorded 4.88 lakhs of people under the category 'Others,' considered to represent the transgender population.

In India, the transgender community is often referred to by terms such as Hijras, Kothas, or Kinnars continues to be marginalized and viewed as societal outcasts. Society rarely acknowledges or empathizes with the immense psychological and emotional distress endured by transgender individuals, particularly those whose gender identity conflicts with their biological sex. Instead, the community faces ridicule, abuse, and exclusion, often being treated as untouchables. The root of their suffering and exclusion lies in society's reluctance to accept diverse gender identities and expressions. A rigid, traditional mindset has relegated the transgender community to society's fringes.

The transgender community faces numerous unique challenges, including unmet healthcare needs, social stigma, lack of awareness, and systemic gatekeeping. In reality they are often denied fundamental rights guaranteed to all Indian citizens, such as the Right to Personal Liberty, Freedom of Expression, Right to Education, and protection against discrimination, exploitation, and violence. Discrimination remains a significant issue for transgender individuals, who are frequently barred from accessing public services and spaces such as schools, hospitals, restrooms, and parks. Private entities often exploit their autonomy to exclude transgender people entirely from their premises. Basic respect and common courtesy are frequently denied, and there is a stark absence of representation to advocate for their rights and social justice. Transgender individuals are often subjected to physical, verbal, and, in extreme cases, sexual abuse, forcing some into commercial sex work. This vulnerability also exposes them to risks such as human trafficking and a higher likelihood of contracting HIV/AIDS.

This study aims to find the barriers preventing transgender individuals from living as ordinary citizens. Its primary objective is to understand the difficulties faced by transgender individuals. Specifically, it seeks to examine their socio-demographic conditions, identify health-related challenges, analyse obstacles in pursuing higher education and employment, and assess their awareness of various government schemes and services offered at both central and state levels.

REVIEW OF LITERATURE

Dutta S., Khan S., and Lorway R. (2019) carried out field research on the structural violence experienced by the Jogappas community in Karnataka. Their study, titled "Following the Divine: An Ethnographic Study of Structural Violence among Transgender Jogappas in South India," was published in the Journal of Culture, Health, and Sexuality. The primary goal of the research was to explore the severe social hardships endured by the lesser-known transgender group, Jogappas, and to examine the intersecting forms of discrimination they face. The study involved observing the daily lives of 80 Jogappas across six towns and villages, along with conducting in-depth interviews with 41 members of the community. The findings revealed that societal forces perpetuate deprivation and exclusion through established social institutions. Despite these challenges, Jogappas demonstrate resilience by forming strong communal bonds with other transgender individuals to confront and resist various forms of social oppression.

Pandya A.K. and Redcay A. (2021) conducted a study titled "Access to Health Services: Barriers Faced by the Transgender Population in India," which was published in the Journal of Gay and Lesbian Health. The research aimed to critically evaluate existing literature on the distinct healthcare needs of transgender individuals, the obstacles they encounter in accessing healthcare, and priorities for medical intervention. The study employed a scoping review methodology, analyzing peer reviewed publications from three databases: PubMed, PsycINFO, and Google Scholar. A total of 67 reports were reviewed, and the findings identified key barriers, including discrimination in healthcare settings, absence of standardized treatment protocols, low health literacy, and limited healthcare-seeking behavior among transgender individuals.

Leppel K. (2021) conducted a study, published in the Journal of Homosexuality, titled "Transgender Men and Women in 2015: Employed, Unemployed, or Not in the Labour Force." The research was based on data from the 2015 US Transgender Survey, the largest sample of transgender individuals to date. The study revealed both high labor force participation and high unemployment rates among transgender men and women. However, transgender women were more likely to be out of the labor force and less likely to secure employment. It highlighted an additional labor market disadvantage faced by transgender individuals, compounded by the existing gender penalty for being female. Although perceived gender congruence was more prevalent among transgender women, its correlation with labor force participation was found to be stronger for transgender men. The study found no evidence that state-level employment non-discrimination laws had a positive impact on labor market outcomes for transgender individuals.

METHODOLOGY

This descriptive study included respondents from three districts Chennai, Chengalpet, and Kanchipuram of Tamil Nadu, India. The sampling method used for the research was Convenient Sampling, a Non-probability sampling method. The samples were selected based on the accessibility and not purposefully and strategically. The sample size of the research was 160. All the samples were transwomen.

MAJOR FINDINGS

Forty-eight percent (48%) of the respondents were of the age group 18-30 years and thirty-four percent (34%) of the respondents were of the age group 31-40 years. Nineteen percent (19%) of the respondents were married. Sixteen percent (16%) were illiterates and more than half of the respondents, fifty-six percent (56%) had dropped out of school. Seventy-five percent (75%) of the respondents were panhandlers. Nineteen percent (19%) of the respondents were Below the Poverty Line (BPL) and thirty-five percent (35%) of the respondents were below the Global Poverty Line as fixed by the World Bank. Six percent (6%) of the respondents were migrants.

Seventy-one percent (71%) of the respondents reported that they were physically healthy. Seventy-three percent (73%) of the respondents reported that they derive benefits through the SMILE Identity Card issued by the Central Government. Ninety-five percent (95%) of the respondents were unaware of the PM-Daksh Programme.

All the respondents received adequate social support. Friends were the most supportive and family were the least supportive. All of them reported that they were aware of the State Government's free bus travel service and have availed the service. Majority of them have the Identity Card issued by the State Government and they were aware of the services provided. The awareness and active participation by the respondents are attributed to the overall usefulness of the State and Central Government ID Cards and the relevant schemes and services. None were aware of the Government Employment portal. Almost all respondents have utilized the common services from the Non Government Organisations such as financial assistance, community programmes, medical camps and emergency assistance during safety concerns.

In this study it was found that in general for all the respondents' income sources were unstable and varied from day to day. Even those in formal employment faced job insecurity and felt compelled to remain inconspicuous in their workplaces to avoid unwanted attention. Transgenders who were into commercial sex work had to remain constantly vigilant, particularly when dealing with law enforcement. In public spaces, they were subjected to discriminatory behavior, with people expressing discomfort and keeping their distance.

CONCLUSION

The hypothesis testing revealed that the respondents reported relatively good physical health, their mental health was found to be below average. Those employed in formal jobs enjoyed a better work environment and faced less discrimination than panhandlers and those into commercial sex work, despite earning comparable or even lower incomes. Despite the challenges they faced in accessing education, respondents expressed hope that the education is significant in improving their future. Although most respondents were aware of government schemes offered by both central and state governments, few were actually getting the maximum benefit from them.

REFERENCES

1 Dutta S., Khan S., and Lorway R., 2019. Following the Divine: an Ethnographic Study of Structural Violence among Transgender Jogappas in South India. Culture. Health & Sexuality, 21(11), pp.1240-1256.

2 Pandya, A.K. and Redcay, A., 2021. Access to Health Services: Barriers faced by the Transgender Population in India. Journal of Gay & Lesbian Mental Health, 25(2), pp.132-154.

3 Leppel, K., 2021. Transgender Men and Women in 2015: Employed, Unemployed, or not in the Labor Force. Journal of Homosexuality, 68(2), pp.203- 229.

10. Religio-philosophical foundation as a coping mechanism for Exile: A Case Study of Tibetan Refugees

Ms. Shilpa Joseph & Ms. G. K. Rhiya Jency
II PG, Department of International Relations,
Loyola College, Chennai

INTRODUCTION

The philosophy underlying every religion explains its ideas, practices, beliefs, and arguments. The philosophical framework guiding each religion justifies the supernatural and divine origin theories. Concepts explained by philosophers of religion include miracles, religious language and belief, concepts of God / Ultimate Reality, religious diversity, arguments for and against the existence of God, suffering, and problems of evil.

A school of thought called logical positivism, which came to be called verificationism, questioned the vagueness and abstract language of religious ideas that were supposed to be labelled 'mysteries'. However, certain analytic philosophers, Basil Mitchell, and H. H. Farmer, revived a continued religious discourse and debate on religious language and concepts.

Another crucial lens for studying religion as a philosophy is realism and neo-realism. While realism looks objectively at religious beliefs, neo-realists explain the concepts in a different setting. Religion is a human creation, and religious language refers to human actions and experiences. There is a perpetual debate about analysing religion, some look for rational justification for religious beliefs, which it often lacks. In contrast, others claim that religion does not require evidence and justification as it is about faith and trust, not evidence.

Religious relativism posits that the truth of a religion is relative to the worldview of its community, acknowledging that different traditions have incompatible yet valid truth claims based on distinct experiences.

Religious exclusivism asserts that only one religion holds the ultimate truth and that conflicting claims from other religions are false, leading to real and intractable disagreements. Critics argue that exclusivism can be seen as arrogant or irrational, raising moral and intellectual objections to its claims.

On the question of the existence of God, philosophers of religion explore diverse conceptions of God or Ultimate Reality. Western traditions (Judaism, Christianity, Islam) typically view it as a personal, omnipotent creator, while Eastern traditions (Buddhism, Taoism, Advaita Vedanta) understand it as an undifferentiated Absolute Reality beyond personal attributes. These differing views influence beliefs about salvation, life after death, and the nature of evil and suffering. A contemporary perspective, known as "ultimism," posits a metaphysical and axiological ultimate reality that is neither theistic nor pantheistic, emphasizing faith in the existence of an ultimate good.

The problem of evil challenges the coexistence of an omnipotent and omnipresent God with the simultaneous existence of evil and pain in the world. Philosophers like David Hume have articulated this dilemma, suggesting that if God is both willing and able to prevent evil, its existence raises questions about His nature. To the paradox of the presence of God and a contradictory force of evil that is thriving together, many theists argue that this conflict can be resolved by suggesting that free will and the potential for moral growth justify the presence of evil. Responses to this issue include defences, which argue that logical incompatibility is not necessary, and theodicies, which seek to explain God's purpose in allowing suffering.

Non-theistic religions like Hinduism and Buddhism address evil and suffering through the concepts of karma and rebirth, suggesting that individuals reap the consequences of their actions across lifetimes. This framework offers a rationale for inequalities in life circumstances, as they are seen as results of past deeds. However, challenges arise regarding the fairness of eternal cycles of rebirth and the implications for free will, raising questions about moral agency and accountability in a karmic system.

Religion as Philosophy as a Coping Mechanism for Refugees

Buddhism

After recognizing the actual extent of suffering in the world, Buddha started to formulate his teachings. Specifically, he understood that everything he held dear would inevitably perish, including himself, due to human death. However, there are other forms of sorrow in life outside death. Buddha held that desire, envy, fear, and other emotions cause human suffering from birth (for both the mother and the child) and throughout life. Additionally, he thought that everyone was destined to continue this cycle indefinitely after being reincarnated in samsara.

Buddhist teaching therefore seeks to end this cycle. The "Four Noble Truths" provide a more thorough explanation of Buddha's methodology:

1. Life carries along with it, suffering.

2. Craving is the main cause of suffering.

3. Suffering ends when the craving comes to an end.

4. One can choose to follow the path that leads him away from craving and suffering. The Tibetan Exile

Tibet has a rich and complex history dating back to at least 127 BCE. It was under the centralised rule of the Tibetan Empire in its imperial age, during the 7th century led by Songtsen Gampo. During his reign between 600 and 650 CE, Tibet was first established as an independent kingdom, and the teachings of Gautama Buddha started to shape Tibet. Tibet used to influence neighbouring countries and, subsequently, came under the influence of powerful foreign rulers like the Manchu emperors, the Mongols, the Gorkhas, and later the British colonial rulers from India. Although Tibet remained an independent sovereign state for centuries, China claims the influence of the Mongol and Manchu empires in the 13th and 18th centuries, to capture the Tibetan land today.

Since 1368, The Ming Dynasty, which took control of China, hardly held any control over Tibet. However, in 1644, the Manchu kings captured China and established the Qing dynasty in the 17th century. During this period, they formed a close relationship with Tibetans, especially through Tibetan Buddhism. The Dalai Lama, the leader of the religious and political community, agreed to be the spiritual mentor for the emperor, creating a “priest-patron” relationship. This was the main connection between Tibet and the Manchus, but it didn’t take away Tibet’s independence.

Between 1720 and 1792, some powerful Manchu emperors, like Kangxi, Yongzheng, and Qianlong, sent their troops to protect the Dalai Lama and his people from threats. These military actions allowed the Manchus to influence Tibetan politics, especially in foreign relations. The Manchu influence was short-lived. When the British invaded Tibet in 1904, their power had further weakened, and it completely ended with the fall of the Qing dynasty in 1911. After that, their connection was broken, marking the end of Manchu control over Tibet.

Despite pressure from China, Britain, and the United States of America, Tibet remained independent and neutral during World War II from I911 to I950. The majority of the neighboring countries maintained diplomatic representatives with the Tibetan government, which in turn had

autonomous foreign relations with them. The People’s Liberation Army (PLA) of the PRC first entered the country in 1949. In May I951, the Tibetan government was forced by the PRC to sign the "I7-Point Agreement for the Peaceful Liberation of Tibet" after defeating the small Tibetan army. Because of the 40,000 Chinese troops stationed and the possibility of a quick occupation of Lhasa, Tibet did not have much options. Viewing the high possibility of the destruction of the Tibetan state, several nations made declarations in the UNGA recognising Tibet’s Independence.

Tibet, during the invasion of China, witnessed strong Chinese communist propaganda wiping away the richness of Tibetan culture and heritage. With the Chinese power over the region, open resistance to their oppression peaked and ultimately led to the fleeing of the Dalai Lama to India. According to anecdotes from Tibetan refugees in India, their ancestors who fled to seek refuge in India, were spread across the country and were provided with strips of land, to make their dwelling. The central Tibetan settlement in Dharamshala, flourished to now become the Buddhist capital. The early refugees engaged in field and plantation labour to make ends meet. Even Buddhist monks used to work in the fields during the day while retreating to meditation and their spiritual exercises later in the evening.

During this period of exile, and in the following 20 years, there was brutal oppression of Tibetan culture and their practice of Buddhism. The Tibetan government in exile estimates that Chinese policies killed more than 1.2 million Tibetans or one-fifth of the population. Tibetans describe the destruction and looting of almost 6000 monasteries, temples, and other historic and cultural structures as a "cultural genocide."All these factors explain the growing Tibetan refugee diaspora across the world.

Tibetan Buddhism and the Refugees

The Buddhist ideas that penetrated Tibet in the 8th century formed their variations with new concepts. Tibetan Buddhism preserves the Mahayana philosophy and cosmology as well as the Theravada teachings, meditation practices, and ordination vows. According to Tibetan Buddhism, enlightenment and everyday life (samsara) are inextricably linked. Tibetan Buddhism stands out for its numerous spiritual development methods and approaches as well as its significant spiritual journey acceleration. The Tibetan Buddhist tradition places great importance on the lama, which is the Tibetan equivalent of the Sanskrit word guru. These gurus are often referred to as Rinpoche, which means "Precious One," in an honorific manner. All lamas must complete a rigorous course of study to prepare them for their future role as providers of initiations and esoteric teachings.

The plight of the refugees was often met by the philosophical assurance that Buddhism provides to the Tibetans. The Tibetans in exile follow their spiritual leader, Dalai Lama in the hope of a deeper spiritual enlightenment. Like any other refugee, the Tibetans always aspire to go back to their homeland, but they focus on a higher goal of preserving their identity and culture through their religious practices in Tibet in exile. The Tibetans follow the Buddhist principles of Kindness, compassion, and non-attachment to material things. They even refrained from violent means of warfare to defend their land and chose to follow a peaceful path of non-violence. They firmly believe in the afterlife in which they keep all their hope. They believe that the years of suffering on earth are for a purpose in the afterlife. This philosophical idea that Buddhism provides makes them rich in heritage and culture although being in exile. They are currently a very successful refugee group in the world.

"This is my simple religion. There is no need for temples; no need for complicated philosophy. Our own brain, our own heart is our temple; the philosophy is kindness." - Dalai Lama

REFERENCES

1. Ashcroft, R. (2022, September 17). Is Buddhism a Religion or a Philosophy? TheCollector. https://www.thecollector.com/buddhism-philosophy-religion/.

2. Imagining home: the reconstruction of Tibet in exile - Forced Migration Review. (2024, August 27). Forced Migration Review. https://www.fmreview.org/harris-2/.

3. International Campaign for Tibet. (2023). Tibetan History. International Campaign for Tibet. https://savetibet.org/why-tibet/history/.

4. Mayer, J.-F. (2007). Introduction: "In God have I put my Trust Refugees and Religion. Refugee Survey Quarterly, 26(2), 6–11. https://www.jstor.org/stable/45054198.

5. Reporter, S. (n.d.). Tibet, Tibetan Refugees and the Way Ahead. Central Tibetan Administration. https://tibet.net/tibet-tibetan-refugees-and-the-way-ahead/.

6. Sakya Monastery of Tibetan Buddhism. (2013). Intro to Tibetan Buddhism. Sakya.org. https://www.sakya.org/resources/intro-to-tibetan-buddhism/.

7. Tibetan Philosophy | Internet Encyclopedia of Philosophy. (n.d.). https://iep.utm.edu/tibetan.

11. கோத்தகிரி பழங்குடி மக்களின் எண்ணம் எழுத்தாதல்

முனைவர் சி. முத்துகந்தன், உதவிப் பேராசிரியர்,
தமிழ்த்துறை, சென்னைக் கிறித்தவக் கல்லூரி

பொதுவாக, பயணங்கள் தான் நம்முடைய தூரங்களைக் கடக்கவும் நமக்கே நம்மீது நெருக்கத்தை உண்டு பண்ணவும் துணை செய்யும். பயண அனுபவம் மட்டுமே நமக்குப் புதிய நபர்களைப் புதிய இடங்களைப் புதியச் சூழலை அமைத்துத் தரும். அதன்வழி ஓர் இனத்தை அல்லது பண்பாட்டை அறிகிற அறிவை இது இயல்பாய் நமக்குக் பெற்றுத்தரும். அந்தவகையில் “இயல்பை அறிதலின் வழி உள்ளுணர்வை எழுத்து வடிவில் வெளிக் கொணர்தல்” என்கிற நோக்குடன் தொடர்ந்து படைப்பாக்கப் பயிற்சிப் பட்டறைகள் நிகழ்த்தப்படுகிறது. இவ்வாறே அக்டோபர் 19 மற்றும் 20 (2024) தேதிகளில் கோத்தகிரி கீஸ்டோன் அறக்கட்டளைச் சார்பாக இருளர், குறும்பர், ஈழவர், ஊராளி மாதிரியான பழங்குடி மக்கள் மத்தியில் நிகழ்த்தப்பெற்ற நிகழ்வு என்பது தனிச்சிறப்பு. பள்ளி / கல்லூரி மாணவரிடையே கிடைக்கும் அனுபவத்தை விட இங்கு மக்களிடமிருந்து கிடைப்பது முற்றிலும் வேறான அசல் அனுபவமாகிறது. இங்கு அனுபவப் பகிர்தலே ஆய்விற்கான களங்களாகக் கொள்ளப்படுகிறது.

கோத்தகிரி பழங்குடி மக்களின் எண்ணம் எழுத்தாதல் எனும் பயிற்சியில் மக்கள் (பங்கேற்பாளர்கள்) எழுதும் சிறு சிறு குறிப்பும் வியப்பைத் தந்தது எனலாம். அவர்களது தெய்வங்களாக கருப்பராயர், பசுவனல்லா, முத்தையா, மண்ணுப்பிள்ளை, மசனிபசுவனல்லா, ஈமாஸ்த்தி, நஞ்சுண்டன், பசேஸ்வரர், அரங்கநாதர், முருகன், மாதேஸ்வரன், ஆலமலை அய்யன், மயிலாடிமாரியம்மன் எனும் தெய்வங்களைக் குறிக்கின்றனர். அவர்களுடைய அப்பா மற்றும் தாத்தாவின் பெயர்களாக மருதன், குன்மாரி, நஞ்சன், சின்னன், மூக்கசாமி, சீரங்கன், ஆண்டியப்பன், ராமன், பத்திரன், மசனன், செல்லன், புலையன், மொண்டிவீரன், ரங்கன், வேலன், தாசன், வெள்ளை, கந்தன், பழனி, நடேசன், நேசன், ஈரன், சித்தன், கோட்டி, மயிலாடி, லட்சுமணன், குன்னன், பண்டன், சீசன், மாரி, ஆறுமுகம், கருப்பையா, மாயன், மொள்ளெ,

கொட்டி, தயாளன், பெருமாள் பெயர்களைப் பதிவு செய்கின்றனர். மருதியம்மாள், பெள்ளி, நீலி, மாரே, பாலி, பத்ரி, காளியம்மா, சிக்கிலி, பொன்னம்மாள், மரக்காள், கெம்பி, புலத்தி, சித்தி, ரேசி, ருக்மணி, கரியள், ரங்கி, பாப்பா, சின்னாத்தாள், பிச்சாய், பொம்மி, மாசி, சிவம்மா. கௌரி, குஜ்ஜி, பத்மினா, ஆச்சி, நீலம்மாள், வேதியம்மாள், மாரை, தேளி, மாரே, கண்ணம்மாள், பொன்னு என்கிற பெயர்கள் அவர்களது அம்மா மற்றும் பாட்டிகளின் பெயர்களாகிறது.

பயிற்சிப் பட்டறை குறிப்பாகப் புனைகதை படைப்பிற்கான களமாகும் ஆனால் பயிற்சியில் எழுதும் அவர்களது எழுத்துகள் அவர்களை அறியாமலே பல்வேறு தரவுகளைக் கொண்டதாக அமைகின்றது. இங்கு பட்டறையின் நோக்கம் என்பது பங்கேற்பாளர்களின் உள் உறைமமாக (INNATE) இருக்கும் படைப்பாற்றலை வெளிக் கொணர்தல். அவர்களுடைய வாழ் சூழலின் அழகியலை உலகிற்கு உணர்த்துதல். பங்கேற்பாளர்களின் வாழ்வியலிலும் பண்பாட்டு மரபிலும் பொதிந்துள்ள கூறுகளைக் காட்சிப்படுத்துதல். அதன்வழி எளியோரிடத்தும் உயர் பண்பாடுகள் இருப்பதைப் புலப்படுத்துதல். ஊட்டி வளர்த்தல் என்பதற்கு மாறாக ஊறித் திளைத்தல் என்பதைப் பயில்வோருக்கு உணர்த்துதல். இன்னொருவரின் எழுத்தைப் படித்து அதையே ஓதுதல் என்பதற்கு மாற்றாக நம்மிலிருந்து புதிதாகத் தோற்றுவித்தல் என்கிற பயிற்சியைக் கற்றுத் தருதல். பயிலரங்க உரையாடலானது இயல்பாகவே சமூகவியல், உளவியல், சூழலியல், பண்பாட்டியல் அணுகுமுறைகளைக் கொண்டிருப்பதனால் பங்கேற்பாளர்கள் மிக யதார்த்தமாகவே தங்கள் இயல்பான மொழிநடையில் படைப்புகளைத் தருவார்கள் என்பது உறுதி என்றவாறு வரையறுத்துக் கொள்ளப்பட்டது.

பொதுவாகப் படைப்பாக்கப் பயிற்சிப் பட்டறையில் மாணவர்களே பங்கேற்பாளர்கள். இங்கு நல் வாய்பாக கோத்தகிரி பழங்குடி மக்களிடம் பங்கேற்கும் வாய்ப்பு கிடைத்தது. பயிற்சியின் தொடக்கமாக செவ்வாய் கிரகம் குறித்து எழுதும்போது அவர்கள் தங்கள் கவனத்தைச் சிதைக்காது மூன்று அல்லது ஐந்து நிமிடங்கள் தொடர்ந்து எழுத வேண்டும். அப்படி எழுதும்போது

பயிற்றுநர் இடையிடையே ஏதாவது ஒரு பொது செய்தியினை முன்னுக்குப்பின் முரணாகப் பேசி கவனத்தைச் சிதைக்க முயற்சிப்பார். ஆனாலும் அவர்கள் அதனைக் கேட்டும் கேட்காததுபோல் கண்டும் காணாது தொடர்ந்து எழுதுவார்கள். அவர்கள் எழுதி முடிக்கும் முன்னே "எழுதியது போதும் கொடுங்கள்" என்றதும் அனைத்து தாள்களையும் சேர்த்து தருவார்கள். அப்படிக் கோத்தகிரி மக்கள் (பங்கேற்பாளர்கள்) ஒவ்வொருவராக எழுதிய வரிகள் அதாவது "என் உலகத்தில் நான்தான் ராணி. நான் கடவுளானால் எனக்குப் பிடித்த உணவெல்லாமே அங்கு இருக்கும். பசி இல்லாமையை மனிதனுக்கு வரமாகக் கொடுப்பேன். என் உலகத்தில் யாரும் ஏற்றத்தாழ்வு பார்க்க மாட்டார்கள். ஆதிவாசி மக்களை வனத்தில் ரொம்பவும் சுதந்திரமாக இருக்கச் செய்வேன். நான் ராகி, சாமை, அக்கலை, அவரை, கொள்ளு ஆகிய வகைகளை மீட்டெடுப்பேன். அதிகமான மலைகளைப் படைப்பேன். அதில் அருவிகள் நிச்சயம் இருக்கும். அங்கே தேனீக்களையும் வண்டுகளையும் கண்டிப்பாகப் படைப்பேன். அங்கு பிளாஸ்டிக் (பாலித்தீன்) பொருட்களுக்கு அனுமதி இல்லை. அங்கே மனிதர்களுக்கும் இடம் இல்லை. அப்படி இருந்தால், மனிதர்கள் முதலில் காட்டில்தான் இருக்க வேண்டும். அனைவரும் நடந்துதான் போகவேண்டும். நான் காட்டில் விலங்குகளை அதிகமாக உருவாக்குவேன். அங்கே விலங்குகளுக்கும் படிப்பறிவைக் கொடுப்பேன். என்னுடைய உலகத்தில் பெண்களுக்கு மட்டுமே அதிகாரம். அங்கு பஸ், கார் போன்ற எந்தப் போக்குவரத்து வசதியும் இருக்காது. ஒவ்வொரு வீட்டிலும் தோட்டமும் ஆடு மாடுகளும் இருக்கும். அனைத்தும் இயற்கைக்கும் பெண்களுக்கும் கட்டுப்பட்டுத்தான் வாழும். நான் அந்தந்தச் சீசனில் மழை பெய்ய செய்வேன். அங்கே காட்டுமரம், செடி, கொடிகளை நன்றாக வளர வைப்பேன். அங்கு நிறைய பள்ளிகளைக் கட்டுவேன். அதில் அனைவருக்கும் கல்வியைச் சமமாகக் கொடுப்பேன். அங்கே அனைவருக்கும் அனைத்து நிலங்களும் சொந்தம். என் உலகத்தில் எல்லோரும் சமம். எனக்கு இன்று என்ன மீட்டிங் என்றே தெரியாது. இங்கு வந்து பார்க்கும் போதுதான் தெரிந்தது. நாம் கற்பனைகளைக் கதையாக எழுத வேண்டும். எனக்கு எழுதத் தெரியாது சார். அப்படி எழுதினால் தவறுகளே அதிகமாக இருக்கும்" என்று

வெள்ளந்தியாகவும் எழதிக் கொடுப்பார்கள். இக்கூற்றுகளை அப்படியே எழுதியதற்கு நேர் எதிராக வாசித்தலே அவர்களது உள்ளார்ந்த எண்ணமாகும் என்பது வெளிப்படை.

அதேபோல் சில திறவுச் சொற்களை அதாவது அண்ணா, ஆயாவைப் போல விடுபட்ட இடங்களில் தாங்களாகவே அகர வரிசையில் எழுதலாம் என்றதும் அவர்களால் மிக இயல்பாகவே எழுதிவிட முடிகிறது. அதாவது இப்பயிற்சியில் இறுதியில் ஒரு கதை கூடப் பிறந்திருக்கும். பங்கேற்பாளர்கள் பயன்படுத்திய சொற்களைப் போலவே வாசிக்கிற நமக்கும் அதே சொற்களும் சில இடங்களில் வேறு சொற்களையும் நிரப்பத் தோன்றும். "நாம் (அம்மாவின்) (ஆசியால்) வந்தவர்கள். வீட்டில் (இலையில்) சாப்பிடும்போது தானாய் (ஈரத்தில்) அமர்ந்தால், அதற்கும் அப்பாதான் சண்டை போடுவார். விடுமுறையில் (உள்ளூரில்) இருக்கும்போதும் (ஊருக்குச்) சென்றாலும் அப்படித்தான். அவர்கள் (எப்படி) உங்களுக்குள் (ஏதாவது) பிரச்சனையா என்று கேட்பார்கள். அதற்கு அம்மா (ஐயத்துடன்) அமைதி காப்பார். அப்பா (ஒன்றுக்கும்) உதவாத உறவுகள், (ஓட்டை) விழுந்த ஓடத்திற்குச் சமம் என்பார். எதனாலோ அம்மா அடிக்கடி (ஔவையாரை) நினைவுப் படுத்திக் கொண்டே வந்தார் என்றெழுதி, உங்களிடம் இதில் உயிர் இருக்கா என்று கேட்டேன். உங்களுக்கு, ஒற்றை வரி எழுதின ஔவையாரை ஏன் எதற்காக நினைவுபடுத்தினார்? என்கிற கேள்வி எழாமல், முதலில் “இந்தாளு இதில என்னதான் சொல்ல வறாரு” என்று உள்ளுக்குள் திட்டக் கூடத் தோன்றும்... சரிதானே” என்று அவர்களுக்கான எழுத்துப் பணியாகும் கொடுத்ததால் பங்கேற்பாளர்கள் நிச்சயம் எழுதி முடிப்பார்கள். அவர்களை அறியாமலே ஒரே பத்தியில் பல தொடர்களை அமைப்பார்கள். வாசித்துப் பார்க்கும் போது ஒவ்வொன்றும் ஒவ்வொரு விதமாக இருக்கும். சிலர் புதிய தொடர்களை எழுத முனைவார்கள். வாசிக்கிற நமக்கும் இந்தச் சொல்லை இந்தத் தொடரை இப்படி அமைந்திருக்கலாமே என்று யோசிக்கத் தோன்றும்.

ஒரே சொல் இருவர் எழுதுவது என்கிற பயிற்சியில் ரோடு, சாவு, மழை, பிரசவம், கீஸ்டோன், தினை, தேன், சடங்கு, மூப்பன், காப்பி, மீன், கடன், தாமரை, வன உரிமைச் சட்டம், மயில்,

ஊர்கூட்டம், மலை, ஜாதிக்காரர், காளான், ஜீப், மைனா, தங்களைப் பற்றி என்கிற மாதிரியான சொற்களை இருவர் கையாளும் போது இரு வேறு கருத்தாக அமைகிறதைக் காண முடிகிறது. அதாவது ஜீப் குறித்து பங்கேற்பாளர் சத்யா எழுதுகிற போது "ஜிப் என்றால் அது ஒரு வாகனம். ஆனால் எங்கள் கிராமத்திற்கு ஆம்புலன்ஸ். எங்கள் சொந்தக் காரியங்களுக்காகவோ அல்லது அவசரத்துக்கு மருத்துவமனைக்கு நாங்கள் அதிகமாக பயன்படுத்தி இருக்கிறோம். எங்கள் கிராமத்தின் ஜீப் ஓட்டுநர்கள் சம்பத் தாத்தா, மணி அண்ணா, கரியன் அண்ணா ஆகியோரை வாழ்வில் மறக்கவே முடியாது. உடல்நிலை சரியில்லாதவர்களை, கர்ப்பிணி பெண்களை காப்பாற்றி உள்ளார்கள். எங்களிடம் பணம் இல்லாமல் இருந்தாலும் கூட எங்களை பாதுகாப்பாக வீட்டிற்கு அழைத்துச் செல்லுவார்கள். இப்போது சம்பத் தாத்தா உயிரோடு இல்லை. வனவிலங்குகள் அதிகமாக இருப்பதால் ஜீப்பில் தான் எங்களின் பயணம் அதிகமாக இருக்கிறது" என்று எழுதி முடிக்கிறார். "கிராமத்தில் அரசு பேருந்து இருந்தாலும் அவசரகால நேரத்திற்கு நான்கு சக்கர வாகனம் ஆம்புலன்ஸிற்குப் பதிலாக வருகிறது. தார் சாலை மிகவும் பழுதடைந்து உள்ளதால் அவசர காலகட்டத்தில் நான்கு சக்கர வாகனம் தான் முதலில் உதவுகிறது. சில கிராமங்களுக்கு ஆம்புலன்ஸ் உடனடியாக செல்ல முடியாத சூழ்நிலையிலும் நான்கு சக்கர வாகனம் மிகவும் அவசர ஊர்தியாக நடமாடி வருகிறது" என்று பங்கேற்பாளர் வசந்தா எழுதிக் காட்டியதின் வழி காண முடிகிறது, வாசிக்கும்போது நமக்கும் அதன் வித்தியாசம் தெரியும். முதலாமவர் எழுதியதை விட கூடுதல் செய்திகளை எழுத வேண்டும். இன்னும் சிறப்பாக எழுத வேண்டும் என்று இரண்டாம் நபருக்கு இயல்பாகவே தோன்றுகிறது. இங்கு வாசிப்பு தூண்டல் பெறச் செய்து இயல்பாகவே ஊக்கத்தையும் உற்சாகத்தையும் தந்து எழுத வைக்கிறதை நம்முடைய வாசிப்பிலும் உணரலாம். இதேபோல "உங்களுக்கான ஒரு சொல் இதுதான்" ஒருவருக்கு ஒரு சொல் என்று பேருந்து, பூசக்காய், பள்ளிக்கூடம், வண்டு, திருமணம், ஆதிவாசி, யானை, நந்தினியின் வரலாறு என்று சொன்னாலே போதும். அந்தச் சொல்லைப் பார்க்கிற போதோ அல்லது கேட்கிற போதோ அதில்

பங்கேற்பாளர்களுக்கு ஏதோவொரு ஈர்ப்பு உண்டாகும். அவர்கள் எழுத எழுத அவர்களை அறியாமலே அது புதியப் புதியத் தொடர்களாய் அமையும். தாங்கள் சொல்ல வந்த செய்தியை முழுமையாக சொல்லிவிட வேண்டும் என்ற எண்ணமும் அப்பொழுதே அவர்களுக்கு உதிக்கும்.

அடுத்து ஒருநாள் பொதுத் தமிழ் வகுப்பில் ஒரு கதை இப்படியாக நிகழ்ந்தது என்று பயிற்றுநர் எடுத்துச் சொல்லி, இங்கும் கரும்பலகையில் அம்மன் - ஒரு லட்சம் - சுடுகாடு - ஆண் - லட்டு- தண்ணீர் - மிட்டாய் - பெண் - மாதவிடாய் - மலர் - முதல்இரவு - ஆண் - இருள் - காடு - ரோஜா - 50000 - ஏழுமலை - கண்ணீர் - மணி - குழந்தை - இறப்பு என்கிற சொற்களோடு பங்கேற்பாளர்களிடமிருந்தும் ஒன்பது சொற்களையும் சேர்த்து எழுதிக் காட்டுகிறார். இதில் இவர்களின் பெற்றோர்களின் பெயர்கள் மட்டுமல்ல இவர்களின் முன்னோர் பெயர்களும் அடங்கும். எழுதும் போது எழுத்தில் யாருக்கு யார் வேண்டுமானாலும் துணையாகலாம். குறிப்பாக எழுதியதை வாசிக்க வாசிக்க அத்தனை மகிழ்ச்சி பங்கேற்பாளர்களிடம் உண்டாகும். உறவுகளுக்குள் கலப்பு ஏற்படும் போதுதான் உற்சாகம் பிறக்கும். ஒரே சொல்லை ஆண் பெண் எப்படிப் பயன்படுத்துகிறார்கள் என்று அவர்களிடமே அந்தப் பொழுது நிகழ்த்துதலாக மாறுகிறதை அறிய முடிகிறது. அதே போன்று அம்மன் - ஒரு லட்சம் - சுடுகாடு - ஆண் - லட்டு தண்ணீர் - மிட்டாய் - பெண் - மாதவிடாய் - மலர் - கடைசி இரவு - ஆண் - இருள் - காடு - ரோஜா - 50000 - ஏழுமலை - கண்ணீர் - மணி - குழந்தை - இறப்பு போன்ற சொற்களில் பங்கேற்பாளர்களிடமிருந்து பெறப்பட்டது. மேற்சொன்ன இச்சொற்களில் ஒரே ஒரு சொல்லை மாற்றியமைத்துப் பார்த்தால், (முதலிரவுக்குப் பதில் கடைசிஇரவு) எழுதும் தொடர்கள் அனைத்தும் அப்படியே தலைகீழாக மாறிப்போகிறதை வெளிப்படையாகக் காண முடிகிறது. அதாவது இந்தமுறை இவர்களது எழுத்து கடைசிஇரவு என்றே பத்திக் கதைகள் முடிகிறதைக் காண முடிகிறது. மனித மனதின் புனையும் ஆற்றலின் ஏற்ற இறக்கங்களை அதன் இயல்பு மாறாமல் வாசிக்க முடிகிறது. வாசிப்பில் இந்த எழுத்தைக் கொண்டே எழுதியவரின் உளப் பாங்கினையும் ஆராய இப்பயிற்சி வழி வகுக்கிறது.

நம்மிடையே உலாவரும் அத்தனை கதைகளும் யாரோ ஒருவர் இட்டுக் கட்டிச் சொல்லியதுதானே. எழுத்தாக அச்சில் இருக்கும் பெரும்பாலான புராண - இதிகாசங்களில் கூட படைப்பாளர்களின் பெயர்கள் தெளிவாகவே உள்ளதே. இருந்தும் தெரிந்தும் கூட எப்படி ஒரு புனைவு நம் வாழ்வின் பேருண்மையாக ஆனது. குறிப்பாக அரூப தொன்மக் கதைகள் உருவமாக மாறி நிற்பது எவ்வளவு சுவாரஸ்யம். சரி மீண்டும் நாம் புதிய கதைகளை இட்டுக்கட்டி எழுதினால் எப்படி இருக்கும்? கொஞ்சம் முயற்சித்து நீங்களும் எழுதிப் பாருங்கள் என்று சொன்னதும் "ஒரு ஊர்ல ஒரு அம்மா, அப்பா, மகள் வசித்து வந்தனர். இவர்கள் வீட்டில் ஒரு அழகான நாய்க்குட்டியும் வளர்த்து வந்தனர். அந்த நாய்க்குட்டியின் பெயர் ரோசி. அந்தப் பெண் குழந்தையின் பெயர் ரேசி. இந்த நாய்க்குட்டிக்கு ரேசி ஒரு நல்ல தோழியாகப் பழகி வந்தாள். எங்கே போனாலும் நாய்க்குட்டியும் அந்தப் பெண் குழந்தை ரேசியும்தான் சென்று வருவார்கள். ஒருநாள் பக்கத்துக் கிராமத்து உறவினர் வீட்டிற்கு அம்மா, அப்பா, ரோசி, ரேசி நான்கு பேரும் சென்றனர். அக்கிராமத்தில் சிறுத்தையின் தொல்லைகள் அதிகமாக இருந்தது. ஒருநாள் ரேசி அந்த வீட்டிற்குள் தூங்கும்போது, வழக்கம் போல ரோசியைத் திண்ணையில் கட்டி வைத்திருந்தனர். திடீரென அந்தப் பக்கமாக வந்த சிறுத்தை, ரோசியைத் தூக்கிச் சென்று கொன்று தின்றுவிட்டது. மறுநாள் காலையில் எழுந்து, ரோசியை ரேசி வந்து தேடிப் பார்க்கும்போது திண்ணையில் காணவில்லை. ரேசி கதறி ஆர்ப்பாட்டம் செய்தாள். அன்றே அவர்கள் அனைவரும் தங்களின் சொந்த ஊருக்கு வந்து சேர்ந்தனர். ரேசிக்கு தன்னுடைய நாய்க்குட்டியின் ஞாபகம் வந்து தன்னுடைய சுயநினைவு இல்லாமல், ரோசியைப் போல் அமைதியாக மூளையில் படுத்து கிடந்தாள். அப்பா, அம்மா இருவரும் மிகவும் மோசமான நிலைக்கு ஆளாகிவிட்டனர். திடீரென ஒரு நாள், அந்தப் பெண் குழந்தை ரோசி நாயாகவே மாறிவிட்டாள். அம்மா, அப்பா இருவரும் தங்களின் மனதைத் தேற்றிக்கொண்டு, இனிமேல் நமக்கு ரோசி, ரேசி இரண்டுமே ஒன்றுதான் என்று நினைத்துக் கொண்டனர். அதிலிருந்துதான் நாய், பூனையை மக்கள் அதிகம் நேசிக்க ஆரம்பித்தார்கள்- C.வசந்தா" என்று எழுதுவதன் மூலம் தெளிவுபட நோக்க முடிகிறது.

மேற்சொன்ன பயிற்சியின் இறுதி நிகழ்வாக அடுத்து குறுங்கதையா! அதெப்படி என்று யோசிக்க வேண்டாம். சிறுகதையைப் போல மிகச் சிறிய கதையிது அவ்வளவுதான் என்றதும் பங்கேற்பாளர்கள் மிக எளிதாக எழுதி முடிக்கிறார்கள். எப்படி இந்த எழுத்துகள் தம்மளவில் பயணித்து பயணித்து இப்படிக் கதையாக ஆனது. தொடர் பயிற்சியே நம்மை அதுவாக்கும் என்பது உண்மைதான். இங்கு கதை சொல்ல வந்தவர்கள் தங்கள் எழுத்தில் இதனைச் சாத்தியமாக்கி இருக்கிறார்கள். ஒருவருக்கொருவர் அக்கதைகளை வாசித்துக் காட்டும் போது, தங்களுக்குள் திருத்திக் கொள்ள ஏதுவாகவும் இருக்கிறது. பங்கேற்பாளர் ராணி அவர்கள் உண்மை கதையில் “ஓர் ஊரில் ஓர் இளம் பெண் இருந்தாள். அவள் பெயர் வள்ளி. வயது ஒன்பது இருக்கும். அவளுக்குத் திருமணம் என்றாலே பிடிக்காது. தாய் தந்தையின் வார்த்தைக்காக அவள் திருமணம் செய்து கொண்டாள். அவளுக்கு மூன்று பெண் குழந்தைகள். சில காலம் கடந்து போனது. குடும்ப சூழ்நிலை காரணமாக தனது கணவரைப் பிரிய வேண்டியிருந்தது. அவளின் மனநிலை பெண் குழந்தைகளை வளர்ப்பது பற்றி தான். பல கஷ்டங்களைத் தாண்டி, தனது மூன்று பெண் குழந்தைகளையும் வளர்த்து விட்டாள். ஒருநாள் வள்ளியின் இரண்டாவது பெண் குழந்தை எனது அப்பா யார்? அவர் எங்கு இருக்கிறார்? அவரை நான் பார்க்க வேண்டும் என்று கேள்வி கேட்கத் தொடங்கினாள். திகைத்து நின்ற தாய், தனது கணவரைப் பற்றி கூறினாள். அவள் கூறியதைக் கேட்ட மகள், தனது தந்தையின் நிலை அறிந்து கொண்டாள். அப்பா இல்லாமல் வாழ்வது என்பது மிகவும் கஷ்டம் என்பதை உணர்ந்தாள். அம்மாவின் கஷ்டங்களைப் பிள்ளைகள் புரிந்து கொண்டார்கள்” என்று எழுதிக் கொடுத்தார். ஆக சிறுகதை என்றால் அதற்கொரு வரையறை இருக்கிறது. கல்விப் புலத்தில் படைப்பிற்கும் கூட சில பல விளக்கங்கள் தரப்படுகிறது. இங்கு எளியவர்கள் எழுதும் எழுத்துகளே அசலானவை இயல்பானவை. இதில் கல்விப்புலம் சார் இலக்கியத் தரத்தை இவர்களிடம் எதிர்பார்த்தல் ஏமாற்றமளிக்கும். பயிற்சிப் பட்டறையின் மைய நிகழ்வு சிறுகதை எழுதுதல். இவை எளிய மக்களின் ஆரம்ப நிலைதான்.

தொடர்ந்து இவர்கள் எழுதுவார்கள் என்றால், நிராகரிக்க முடியாத பல படைப்புகள் இங்கிருந்து வரும் என்பதே உண்மை.

இறுதியாக இப்பயிற்சியின் நோக்கம் படைப்பாக்கம் என்றாலும் இச்சமூகத்திற்குக் கல்வி எவ்வளவு முக்கியம் என்பதைப் பங்கேற்பாளர்கள் கூறியிருப்பார்கள். "எவ்வளவு கஷ்டப்பட்டாலும் கடைசியில் நல்லா படிச்சு நல்ல நிலைமைக்கு வரனும். பள்ளிக்கூடத்துக்கு ரொம்ப தூரம் நடந்து போய்தான் படிக்கணும், வழியில நிறைய நிறைய தடைகள் இருந்தாலும் அதை உடைச்சிட்டுதான் படிக்கப் போகணும். ஒரு பெண்ணுக்குப் படிப்பு எவ்வளவு முக்கியம் என்பதை உணர்ந்து நல்லா படிக்கணும். படித்து நல்ல நிலைமைக்குப் போகணும். பெத்தவங்கள காப்பாத்தணும். எங்களுக்கு இருந்த சோகங்கள எல்லாம் நாங்கள் தீர்த்துக்கிட்டோம்" இப்படியாகக் கல்வி மீதான அவர்களின் ஏக்கம் சில கதைகளில் வெளிப்பட்டுள்ளது. எத்தனை இடர்கள் வந்தாலும் அவர்களின் வாழ்க்கையின் முக்கிய அங்கமாக கல்வியை வைத்திருக்கின்றனர்" என்று இவர்கள் எழுதியிருப்பது கோத்தகிரி பழங்குடி மக்களின் எண்ணம் மட்டுமல்ல எளியவர்கள் அத்தனைப் பேரின் எண்ணமும் கல்வியைப் பெறுவதே என்பது இதன்வழி புலனாகிறது.

துணைநூல் பட்டியல்

1. இரா. கிருத்துதாசு காந்தி, தமிழ்நாட்டு ஆன்றோர்கள் (ST), பாலம், சென்னை, 2024.

2. ம. இராசேந்திரன், மெக்கன்சி சுவடிகளில் தமிழகப் பழங்குடிகள் மக்கள், அடையாளம், திருச்சி, 2016.

3. தமிழ்நாடன் (தொ. ஆ), தமிழ்நாட்டு மலைவாழ் பழங்குடி மக்கள், சேலம் மாவட்ட ஓவியர் எழுத்தாளர் மன்றம், சேலம், 1996.

4. ப. சண்முகசுந்தரம், தமிழர் தமிழ்நாட்டின் பழங்குடிகள், மணிவாசகர் பதிப்பகம், 2017.

5. இருளர்க்கும் பகலுண்டு, சிறு வெளியீடு, பாலம், சென்னை.

12. A Study on Emotional Well-being of the Elderly Women

Ms. Sharon Mary Rajesh, I MSW, Children and Families, Madras School of Social Work,
Ms. Hafiza Abdul Khader, I MSW HRM, D.G. Vaishnav College &
Dr. A. Sylvia Daisy Associate Professor, Department of Social Work, Self Financed Stream, Madras Christian College

INTRODUCTION

The traditional joint family system in India once provided emotional, social, and financial support for the elderly, fostering their well-being and integrating them into family life. However, the rise of nuclear families, driven by industrialization, urbanization, and the one-child norm, has significantly altered caregiving practices. This shift has led to an increasing number of elderly individuals, particularly women, being institutionalized in old age homes. This study examines the emotional well-being of elderly women residing in residential care facilities in Trivandrum and Hosur, exploring their experiences of loneliness, perceived abandonment, and diminished roles in society. It poses the critical question: Should we return to traditional joint family structures to address the emotional needs of the elderly? Elderly care in India has traditionally been rooted in the joint family system, where elders were valued as the custodians of wisdom, culture, and traditions. They held significant roles as decision-makers and advisors, and their emotional and physical needs were met by their children and grandchildren. This arrangement fostered a sense of belonging and reduced the likelihood of social isolation and loneliness.

However, with the onset of industrialization and the migration of younger generations to urban areas, the structure of Indian families has shifted. The nuclear family, characterized by smaller households and fewer intergenerational interactions, has become the norm. The rise of the one-child family, coupled with the increasing demands of modern life, has further reduced the capacity of families to care for their elderly members. As a result, many elderly individuals, particularly women who often outlive their spouses, find themselves placed in residential care facilities or old age homes. While these institutions provide essential services, they often fail to meet the emotional and social needs of their residents. This study focuses on the experiences of elderly women in residential care facilities at Trivandrum and Hosur, examining the impact of institutionalization on their emotional well-being and exploring potential solutions to this growing societal challenge.

METHODOLOGY

Descriptive design was adopted to explore the emotional well-being of elderly women in residential care facilities. The study was conducted in Trivandrum, Kerala and Hosur, Tamil Nadu, two cities with distinct socio-cultural contexts. A total of 50 elderly women, aged 60 years and above, were selected through random sampling, with 25 participants from each city. Data was collected through Interview Schedules with closed and open-ended questions. The Warwick Edinburgh Mental Well-being Scale (WEMWBS) measured positive mental health and psychological functioning and the BBC Subjective Well-being Scale (BBC-SWB) measured life satisfaction and happiness. The interview schedule focused on various aspects of the participants' lives, including their experiences of institutionalization, their relationships with family members, and their perceptions of emotional and social well-being. The data was analyzed thematically to identify common patterns and differences in the experiences of elderly women in the two residential care facilities.

FINDINGS

The participants in this study were predominantly widows. Many of the women had limited formal education and were financially dependent on their families before being placed in residential care. Their transition from a family setting to an institutional environment was often driven by a combination of factors, including the migration of their children, financial constraints, and the inability of family members to provide adequate care at home. Majority of the participants had previously lived in joint family households. This transition marked a significant change in their roles and identities, as they moved from being respected elders within their families to becoming residents in an institutional setting. Trivandrum residential care facility has a higher proportion of elderly women with no family members (20%) and with larger families of 5-8 members (24%) than Hosur (0%) respectively. Hosur has a higher proportion of elderly women who felt abandoned by their families due to the transition from a joint family system to a nuclear family system (20%) than Trivandrum (80%).

In Hosur, the most common wish was to live happily with family, as 40% of them expressed this desire. Other wishes included having a family of their own, travelling, success of family members, shopping, and being healthy, each reported by 4% to 8% of the respondents. A significant segment (32%) reported having no wishes at all. None of them wished to see their family at least once, go on a pilgrimage, have a peaceful death, marry according to their family's choice, or go back in time and change their fate. This reflects that most elderly people in Hosur's residential care facility are content with their current situation and do not have high expectations or regrets. In Trivandrum, the most common wishes were to see their family at least once and to live happily with family, each reported by 20% of the respondents. Other wishes included having a family of their own, travelling, going on a pilgrimage, having a peaceful death, marrying according to their family's choice, and going back in time and changing their fate, each reported by 4% to 16% of the respondents. None of them wished for the success of family members, shopping, or being healthy. This indicates that most elderly people in Trivandrum's residential care facility have unfulfilled desires and aspirations and are not satisfied with their current situation. Thus, the findings suggest that elderly people in both Hosur and Trivandrum have different wishes, but Hosur has more elderly people who are happy with their lives, while Trivandrum has more elderly people who are unhappy with their lives.

In Hosur, more than half (52%) reported being happy, while only 4% were unhappy and 32% had mixed feelings. A small segment (12%) did not know how to answer. This shows that most elderly women in Hosur's residential care facilities enjoy their living conditions and environment. In Trivandrum, less than a third (32%) expressed happiness, while 36% were unhappy and 28% had mixed feelings. Only 4% did not know how to answer. This indicates that most elderly women in Trivandrum's residential care facility are dissatisfied with their living conditions and environment.

Two emotional well-being scales, the Warwick Edinburgh Mental Well-being Scale (WEMWBS) and the BBC Subjective Well-being Scale (BBC-SWB). The data showed that the higher the score, the worse the well-being, and the lower the score, the better the well-being. The data reveals the following patterns: For the WEMWBS, the total score for Hosur is 1016, while for Trivandrum it is 1081. This means that the average score for Hosur is 40.64, while for Trivandrum it is 43.24. This indicates that the elderly people in Hosur have slightly better mental well-being than the elderly people in Trivandrum, according to this scale. For the BBC-SWB, the total score for Hosur is 1149, while for Trivandrum it is 1051. This means that the average score for Hosur is 45.96, while for Trivandrum it is 42.04. This indicates that the elderly people in Hosur have slightly worse subjective well-being than the elderly people in Trivandrum, according to this scale. The data shows a negative correlation between the two scales, meaning that the higher the score on the WEMWBS, the lower the score on the BBC-SWB, and vice versa. This suggests that the two scales measure different aspects of well-being and that positive mental health does not necessarily imply life satisfaction and happiness, and vice versa.

The shift from joint families to nuclear families has significantly influenced the emotional well-being of elderly women. In traditional joint families, elderly members were integrated into the daily life of the household, providing them with a sense of purpose and belonging. However, the rise of nuclear families, driven by economic pressures and changing social norms, has disrupted this dynamic. Many participants in this study expressed feelings of abandonment and neglect by their children, who had moved to urban areas or abroad for work. The physical distance and the demands of their children's careers made it difficult for them to maintain regular contact and provide emotional support. This sense of abandonment was particularly pronounced among the participants in Hosur, where a significant number of women attributed their institutionalization to their children's migration. Those who had strong relationships with their children and received regular visits reported higher levels of emotional well-being compared to those who felt abandoned and neglected.

Based on the findings of this study, several recommendations can be made to improve the emotional well-being of elderly women in residential care facilities:

1. Promote Intergenerational Living: Encourage families to adopt living arrangements that allow elderly members to remain integrated into family life, even if it requires creative solutions such as shared housing or co-living arrangements.

2. Enhance Community Support: Develop community-based programs that provide social engagement opportunities for the elderly, helping to reduce feelings of isolation and loneliness.

3. Strengthen Family Bonds: Encourage families to maintain regular contact with their elderly members, even if they live apart, through phone calls, video chats, and periodic visits.

4. Improve Institutional Care: Enhance the quality of care provided in residential facilities by incorporating social activities, counseling services, and opportunities for meaningful engagement.

5. Advocate for Policy Changes: Advocate for government policies that support families in caring for their elderly members, including financial incentives, caregiving support, and the development of community care networks.

CONCLUSION

The transition from traditional joint families to nuclear families has had a profound impact on the emotional well-being of elderly individuals in India. While institutionalization provides a practical solution for families facing economic and logistical challenges, it often fails to address the emotional and social needs of the elderly. This study underscores the importance of re-evaluating current caregiving practices and exploring alternative models that prioritize the emotional well-being of elderly individuals. Given the findings, it is essential to ask: Should we go back to the same old traditional families? Can a return to the values and practices of joint family systems offer a solution to the emotional distress experienced by the elderly in modern society? By fostering intergenerational connections and strengthening community support, society can create a more inclusive and compassionate environment for its aging population.

REFERENCES

1. Forbes, (n.d.), Residential Care Homes: Benefits, Costs and More - Forbes Health http://www.forbes.com/health/senior-living/care-homes/.

2. Lee, G, &Ishii-Kuntz, M. (1987), Social Interaction, Loneliness, and Emotional Well-being among the Elderly, Research on Aging,459-482, doi:10.1177/0164027587094001.

3. WHO, W. (2023) Mental Health of Older Adults-World health organization (WHO). http://www.who.int/news-room/facts-sheets/detail/mental-health-of-older-adults.

13. A Study on Parenting Style of Single Parents

Mr. Ajay Kumar. R, II MSW HRM & Mr. Mohan Raj. R,
Assistant Professor, Department of Social Work,
Self Financed Stream, Madras Christian College, Chennai

INTRODUCTION

Parenting is a complex process that involves a wide range of skills, knowledge, and behaviors that parents use to raise their children. Parenting styles are often categorized as authoritative, authoritarian, permissive, and neglectful. Single parenthood is becoming more prevalent in today's society due to factors such as divorce, separation, and the choice to have children without a partner. Parenting styles adopted by single parents can have a significant impact on their children's growth and well-being. However, there are unique challenges faced by single parents that may influence their parenting styles. Single parents face numerous challenges that can have an impact on their parenting style, such as limited financial resources, time constraints, emotional stress, and social stigma. These challenges can have a profound effect on how single parents raise their children.

The purpose of this study was to explore the parenting style of single parents registered in selected non-governmental organizations in Chennai district, Tamil Nadu. The study focussed on the difficulties single parents encountered and the parenting strategies they employ to address these difficulties.

Single Parenting

In today's world, single parenting is more prevalent than ever before, and it presents particular difficulties for parents who are raising their children alone. These difficulties may significantly affect the parenting approach used by single parents, which may in turn affect the child's growth, conduct, and general well-being. Limited financial support is one of the major issues single parents confront. It can be difficult and have an effect on both the parent and child's life. As a result of their financial struggles, single parents may find it difficult to meet their children's basic needs, including food, shelter, and education. This can have an impact on the parenting style they choose. Managing job, domestic duties, and parenting are common juggling acts for single parents. They might not have as much time as they would like to spend with their child, which might affect both their bond and the child's growth.

Another issue single parents deal with is emotional stress. They may feel isolated, lonely, and anxious since raising a child alone can be emotionally taxing. They may find it difficult to assist their child emotionally while managing their own emotions, which can have an impact on their parenting. It's possible for single parents to feel insecure and unsure about their capacity to raise their child on their own. They may adopt an overly liberal or overprotective parenting style as a result of their insecurities. They may experience societal shame and discrimination too.

Single parents may encounter judgement and criticism from others since single parenthood is frequently perceived negatively by society. This stigma may have an impact on their parenting approach by lowering their sense of self worth and parental confidence. The aim of this study is to examine the parenting styles and to find the difficulties of single parents and how they affect their parenting practices.

REVIEW OF LITERATURE

In a study titled, "Single-Parent Families and Their Effect on Children, Ramachandran, V. and Kandiah, D. (2017) investigated on how single-parent households affect the social, emotional, academic progress of children and the coping methods single parents employ to raise their children.

A study on "Single Mothers in India: Problems, Coping Strategies and Support Networks" by Desai, N. (2016) focussed on the difficulties faced by single mothers in India, including limited financial resources, social stigma, and a dearth of support systems. Additionally, the study also explored the coping mechanisms employed by single mothers and the assistance provided by NGOs.

A study on "Parenting Styles and Children's Academic Achievement has compared the parenting practices and children's academic success in single-parent families in Chennai. The study highlights the difficulties faced by single parents in relation to the academics of their children.

"Single Mothers in India: Problems and Prospects, published in 2018 by Srivastava, A. and Saxena, N. gives a general summary of the issues of single mothers in India, their experiences, financial difficulties, lack of access to healthcare, education, and social stigma.

METHODOLOGY

This research was a quantitative research in which descriptive research design was adopted. The data was collected from the single parents registered in the Non-Governmental Organisations of Chennai district, Tamil Nadu. The sample size was 50. Cluster Sampling method was adopted for the study. Interview schedule was used as a tool for data collection. The respondents served as the main source of information. The secondary data was collected from books, research articles and the internet respectively. The objectives of the research were to study the demographic details of the respondents, their socio-economic status, social support, and coping mechanisms that affect parenting practices, to know their difficulties in parenting their children and to understand their coping mechanisms, to find how single parenting affects a child's academic performance and health.

MAIN FINDINGS

• Eighty percent of the respondents had become single parents due to the death of the spouse and they have attributed reasons like accidents, coronavirus infection, alcoholism or fatal diseases. A majority of them reported that an authoritative parenting style is good.

• Sixty-four percent (64%) of the respondents were having two children.

• Twenty-four percent (24%) of the respondents were single parents for six to eight years.

• Ninety-eight percent (98%) of the respondents reported that their major role was to raise their children.

• Eighty-eight percent (88%) of the respondents reported that they spend time with their children.

• Seventy-four percent (74%) of the respondents were employed.

• Thirty-two percent (32%) of the respondents were earning a monthly income that ranged from seven thousand to eight thousand and most of them were working in the unorganized sector.

• Seventy percent (70%) of the respondents did not get financial support from the parents and they were self dependent.

• Eighty-four percent (84%) of the respondents did not get financial support from their In -law's family.

• Forty percent (40%) of the respondents had noticed that there were changes among the family members after them becoming single parents.

• Thirty-six percent (36%) of the respondents noticed that there were changes among the known people after becoming single parents.

• Forty-eight percent (46%) of the respondents believed that negative attitudes towards the single parent are on the rise.

• Thirty-eight (38%) percent of the respondents felt emotionally imbalanced sometimes after being a single parent.

• Fifty percent (50%) of the respondents were facing discrimination in the workplace.

• Ninety-eight percent (98%) of the respondents' family had the respondents as the decision maker in their family.

• Fifty-eight percent (58%) of the respondents reported that their children were not happy due to social stigma, being raised by a single parent.

• Eighty-four (84%) percent of the respondents' children understood their responsibility.

• Seventy percent (70%) of the respondents' children's academic performance were good despite being raised by a single-parent.

CONCLUSION

The study highlights how important it is to understand the parenting styles of single parents and how they impact the wellness of their children. It is important for single parents to adopt an authoritative parenting style that emphasizes warmth and control, as this has been found to be the most effective parenting technique for producing excellent results for children. It was found that having children presents a variety of challenges for single parents, such as balancing work and parenting responsibilities, financial issues, and a lack of support from friends and relatives, these challenges affect the parenting styles of single parents. By providing them with financial assistance, emotional support, and parenting education, non-governmental organizations can be of great assistance to single parents.

REFERENCES

1.Gupta A, Kashyap S. One of the factors influencing an adolescent's wellbeing is growing up in a single-parent household. Adv J Soc Sci. 2020;7: 138–44.

2. Mabuza N, Thwala SK, Okeke CIO. The impact of single parenting on Swaziland children's emotional development Mediterr J Soc Sci. 2014;5: 2252.

3. Bhat NA, Patil RR. Single parenthood families and their impact on children in India. Delhi Psychiatry J. 2019;22: 161–5.

4. Kotwal N, Prabhakar B. Challenges encountered by single mothers, J Soc Sci. 2009;21:197–204.

5. Atlas S. Single Parenting. Englewood Cliffs, NJ: Prentice-Hall; 1981.

6. Barry A. A research project on successful single-parent families. Am J Fam Ther. 1979;7: 65–73.

7. Torres L, Taknint J. T. Cultural microaggressions, symptoms of traumatic stress, and depression in Latinos: A model examining moderated mediation. J Couns Psychol. 2015;62: 393–401. [PubMed].

8. Kristenson M, Orth-Gomér K, Kucinskienë Z, Bergdahl B, Calkauskas H, Balinkyniene I, et al. Reduced cortisol response to a standardized stress challenge in Lithuanian compared to Swedish men: The LiVicordia study. Int J Behav Med. 1998; 5:17–30. [PubMed].

9. Lisa BF, Leonard S. Psychosocial Processes and Health: A Reader. Cambridge: Cambridge University Press; 1994. Social Networks, Host Resistance and Mortality: A Nine-Year Follow-up Study of Alameda County Residents; pp. 43–67.

10. Amato PR, Keith B. Parental separation and its impact on children's welfare: A meta-analysis. Psychol Bull. 1991; 110:26–46. [PubMed].

11. Hilton JM, Devall EL. Analysis of parenting styles and children's conduct in single-mother, single-father, and intact families. J Divorce Remarriage. 1998; 29:23–54.

12. Aseltine RH. Pathways linking parental divorce with adolescent depression. J Health Soc Behav. 1996; 37:133–48. [PubMed].

13. Dodge KA, Petit GS, Bates JE. The relationship between child behavior issues and socioeconomic status is mediated by socialization. Child Dev. 1994;65: –65. [PubMed] [Google Scholar].

14. A Study on the Impact of Madras Christian College Family Life Institute on the Health and Socio-Economic Condition of its Beneficiaries

Jessica Jasmine.R, Jenita Mary. F & Dr. A. Sylvia Daisy,
Associate Professor, Department of Social Work,
Self-Financed Stream, Madras Christian College, Chennai

INTRODUCTION

The research work aims to study the impact of Madras Christian College Family Life Institute on health and socio-economic condition of its beneficiaries at Mappedu, Chengalpattu District. The MCC FLI started to function in 1971 providing maternal and child health services to rural women in and around Mappedu village in congruence with the mission of Madras Christian College, "service to humanity". The MCC FLI was registered as a Clinic under the Tamil Nadu Clinical Establishment Act in January 2021. Presently it has two functional units, the MCC FLI Clinic providing basic health services, creating health awareness, conducting medical camps and the MCC FLI Tailoring unit catering to the Socio economic needs of the women residing at Mappedu. Self Help groups, savings and revolving loans, registration of micro enterprises, technical guidance and support are the services rendered through the tailoring unit. MCC FLI has rendered more than fifty years of service to the vulnerable and weaker sections of the nearby rural community.

Understanding the impact of Madras Christian College Family Life Institute (MCC FLI) on the health and socio-economic condition of its beneficiaries is imperative for a multitude of reasons. Moreover, such a study can serve to enhance the outcomes experienced by beneficiaries. By identifying strengths and areas for improvement within MCC FLI's programs, interventions can be tailored to better meet the diverse needs of beneficiaries, thereby improving their overall quality of life. By documenting MCC FLI's experiences and outcomes, this study generates valuable knowledge. By shedding light on MCC FLI's contributions and challenges, this study has the potential to catalyse positive change and improve the lives of individuals and communities served by the institute.

METHODOLOGY

The major objective of the study was to find the impact of Madras Christian College Family Life Institute on the Health and Socio-economic development of the beneficiaries. The specific objectives were to find their level of awareness of the Services of MCC FLI and their level of utilization of the services. MCC FLI caters to all the needy women disregard of their caste and religion. Special care is rendered to the marginalised communities.

The research was centered on the beneficiaries of MCC Family Life Institute focusing on the impact of health and socio-economic development, fifty women beneficiaries above 25 years were selected for the study through Convenience sampling. A descriptive research design was adopted and data was collected through the Interview schedule.

FINDINGS

Demographic details

From data analysis it is interpreted that twenty-six percent (26%) of the respondents were between the age group of 20 -25 years, six percent (6%) were between the age group of 25-30 years, sixteen percent (16%) were between 30-35 years, thirty percent (30%) were between 35-40 years and twenty percent (20%) of them above 40 years.

Seventy-four percent (74%) of the respondents were married, thirty percent (30%) were unmarried, fourteen percent (14%) were separated and two percent (2%) were divorcees. Thus, the majority of the respondents were married.

Twenty-six percent (26%) of the respondents were Scheduled Caste, six percent (6 %) of the respondents were ST, twenty-eight (28%) of the respondent were MBC, twenty percent (20%) of the respondents were BC and twenty percent (20%) of the respondents were OC.

Eighty 80% of the respondents were Hindu, two percent (2%) were Muslim and eighteen percent (18%) were Christians, Thus, the majority of the respondents are Hindu.

Twenty four percent (24%) of the respondents had completed collegiate education thirty six percent (36%) of the respondents had completed higher secondary education, fourteen percent (14%) of the respondents had completed high school education, four percent (4%) of the respondents had completed primary education and twenty two percent (22%) were illiterates.

Level of Awareness of MCC FLI Services

Eighty-two percent (82%) were aware of the MCC FLI clinic services, and the consultation services rendered by the Doctor on every Thursday. Ninety percent (90%) of the respondents were aware of the MCC FLI residential staff nurse and the medical services, Eighty-six percent (86 %) of the respondents were aware of the basic medicines given freely in MCC FLI Clinic. Fifty percent (50%) of the respondents were aware of community awareness programs conducted by MCC FLI. Fifty--our (54%) of the respondents were aware of medical camps conducted by MCC FLI.

Eighty-two percent (82%) of the respondents were aware of the MCC FLI Tailoring unit. Fifty-two percent (52%) of the respondents were aware of the MCC FLI-RRR Skill training program. Forty-six percent (46%) of the respondents were aware of the NSDC Courses offered. Forty-six percent (46%) of the respondents were aware of the MCC FLI-MCC MRF Self Help Groups, savings and revolving loans. Twenty-four percent (24%) of the respondents were aware of the MCC FLI awareness programs in neighbourhood schools. Twenty-six (26%) were aware of the covid relief work of MCC FLI.

Level of Utilisation of MCC FLI Services

Seventy-two percent (72 %) of the respondents utilized MCC FLI Clinic services. Sixty-two percent (62%) of the respondents utilized the doctor consultation on every Thursday. Sixty-six percent (66%) utilised services of the Residential Staff Nurse. Eighty-six percent (86%) of the respondents availed basic medicines given free of cost at MCC FLI Clinic.

Fifty-eight percent (58%) of the respondents utilized the MCC FLI Tailoring unit services. Thirty-four percent (34%)of the respondents utilized the services of MCC FLI-RRR Skill training program. Thirty-four percent (34%) of the respondents utilized services of MCC FLI NSDC Course.

Forty-six percent (46%) of respondents utilized community awareness programs conducted by MCC FLI. Forty-four percent (44%) of respondents benefitted through medical camps of MCC FLI. Thirty-eight percent (38%) benefitted through the MCC FLI-MCC MRF Self Help Groups, small savings and revolving loans. Twenty-six percent (26%) of respondents benefitted from MCC FLI School Awareness programs, twenty-two percent (22%) of respondents benefitted from the Covid Relief work of MCC FLI. Thirty-eight percent (38%) of respondents reported that their parents benefitted from MCC FLI services and forty-four percent (44%) of respondents reported that their children benefited from MCC FLI services.

A comparison of the data relating to level of awareness and level of utilisation shows a significant relationship. When the awareness level was high the utilisation of services was also high. When the lever of awareness of a specific service was low the utilisation was also low. Hence creating awareness of the services through different modes of communication, campaigns, social media etc will help in reaching the unreached. The marginalised need to be educated about the services for better results relating to Social Inclusion and Social Equity.

REFERENCES

1. Goldie Kadushin. Health & social work 29 (3), 219-244, 2004 https://academic.oup.com/hsw/article-abstract/29/3/219/698770.

2. Kadushin G. (2004). Home health care utilization: a review of the research for social work. Health & social work, 29(3), 219–244.

https://doi.org/10.1093/hsw/29.3.219 6. Mayo Clinic College of Medicine and Science. Medical Social Worker - Explore HealthCare Careers. https://college.mayo.edu.

3. CareerExplorer. What does a healthcare social worker do? https://www.careerexplorer.com.

4. Indeed. What Does a Hospital Social Worker Do? (With Specialties). https://www.indeed.com.

5. NASW. Social Workers in Hospitals & Medical Centers https://www.socialworkers.org.

6. Keuka College. Duties of a Social Worker in Healthcare https://onlinedegrees.keuka.edu.

15. Assessing the Efficacy of Assistive Technologies in Improving Communication Skills for People with Multiple Disabilities

Ms. Swetha Anand, II MSW &
Mr. J. P. Francis Dhivakar, Assistant Professor,
Department of Social Work, SFS, Madras Christian College

INTRODUCTION

People with multiple disabilities have serious challenges in developing effective communication skills because of the coexistence of cognitive, sensory, motor, and communication impairments. These barriers limit their social interactions and quality of life. Communication is essential for human beings. Persons with multiple disabilities face problems in the expression of ideas, wants, and emotions.

Studies reveal that assistive technologies such as speech-generating tools, and sensory interfaces are promising, their specific impact on the beneficiaries need to be studied. This study was conducted at NIEPMD in Chennai, focusing on family members, teachers, and professionals who work closely with people with multiple disabilities. The objective was to find the efficacy of assistive technologies in promoting communication skills with the persons with multiple disabilities. Descriptive research design and Convenience sampling were adopted. Number of respondents was thirty.

FINDINGS

Among the respondents 73% agreed on the effectiveness of assistive communication devices in enhancing communication skills for individuals with multiple disabilities, 24% were neutral, only 3% disagreed.

There were mixed opinions about the use of AAC devices for children with multiple disabilities. A total of 46% believed that AAC devices work, while 30% disagreed and 24% were not sure.

Mixed responses were reported about the efficacy of AAC devices in helping children communicate. Respondents reported a mixed perception of speech-generating devices in promoting social interaction for children with communication difficulties, 53% agreed that the device was useful while 43% were neutral and 4% disagreed that it was useful.

There were mixed responses towards the integration of communication assistive technologies in everyday life, 44% expressed difficulties, 26% expressed no difficulty at all, and 30% were uncertain.

There were mixed responses regarding age as a factor having an impact on usage of communication assistive technologies, 57% of respondents agreed that age does impact, 10% of them disagreed, in addition, 33% of the respondents were unsure.

The data indicated that people of younger age groups can easily adapt to communication assistive technologies. The number of respondents agreed with the statement was 57%, whereas 43% were neutral.

Among the respondents 70% reported that they like collaboration with the other stakeholders such as parents, teachers, and therapists, in using these communication assistive technologies, 15% were not willing to collaborate and 15% did not respond.

SUGGESTIONS

To increase access and availability of assistive technologies.

To implement policies to remove barriers to access.

To develop training for educators and healthcare professionals.

To encourage collaboration among parents, teachers, and therapists. ·

To promote usage of assistive technologies in educational institutions.

CONCLUSION

The study highlights the need for greater collaboration among parents, educators, and therapists, as well as the need to upgrade training and awareness about assistive technologies. In addition, easy access and affordability of these technologies along with the emphasis to use the devices in educational institutions can significantly enhance the outcomes for individuals with multiple disabilities. Overall, the study points out that assistive technologies enhance inclusion and aid people in overcoming barriers of communication, which improves their social interactions and quality of life.

REFERENCES

1. Cumley, G. Swanson. S. Augmentative and Alternative Communication,1999 http://doi.org/10.1080/07434619912331278615

2. F Stasolla, AO Caffo, L Picucci, A BoscoAssistive technology for promoting choice behaviors in three children with cerebral palsy and severe communication impairments - 2013

3. A Shay, M Scherer-2019 Assistive technology techniques, tools, and tips https://doi.org/10.1016/B978-0-12-812979-1.00016-3

4. Giulio E. Lancioni, Jeff Sigafoos, Mark F. O'Reilly & Nirbhay N. Singh-2019 Speech Generating Devices for Communication and Social Development

5. N Bianquin, F Sacchi, S Besio -2018 Enhancing communication and participation using AAC technologies for children with motor impairments: a systematic review.

16. A Study on the Impact of Climate Change and Marginalization Experienced by Women

M. V. Akshaya, II MSW HRM & Dr. Baily Vincent,
Associate Professor, Department of Social Work, SFS,
Madras Christian College, Chennai

INTRODUCTION

Climate change is the most urgent concern of the twenty-first century. Geographical, generational, age, class, economic, and gender differences all affect its effects. It is clear from the intergovernmental panel on Climate Change's (IPCC) research that the most impacted individuals would also be the most marginalized and at risk. It is expected to have an impact on both working men and women. But gender is not equally affected by climate change. Since women make up the majority of the world's Impoverished and are disproportionately more reliant on endangered natural resources, they are increasingly perceived as being more vulnerable than men to the effects of climate change as already one of the most marginalized groups in society, women are disproportionately affected by the most destructive effects of climate change. This study emphasizes the urgent need to acknowledge climate change as an intersectional feminist issue and calls for greater representation of women in the development of climate solutions.

A group's systematic exclusion from the socio-economic and political arenas, which restricts their access to opportunities, resources, and decision-making processes, is referred to as marginalization. Compounded disadvantages result from the intersection of this exclusion with other characteristics like gender, ethnicity, and economic status. Climate change refers to substantial, long-term changes in the weather patterns of the world, which are mostly caused by human activities such as the burning of fossil fuels and deforestation. Increased frequency of extreme weather events, rising sea levels, and rising temperatures are some of its manifestations that disproportionately affect vulnerable populations and exacerbate pre existing vulnerabilities.

Women's lives, particularly those in rural or underprivileged areas, are severely affected by the junction of marginalization and climate change. The majority of the world's impoverished are women, and they depend significantly on natural resources to support themselves. Due to environmental degradation, they are forced to go for supplies farther away, which puts them at higher danger of sexual harassment and assault as well as injuries from long-distance lugging of heavy burdens. Moreover, women are disproportionately affected by climate related displacement, accounting for 80% of those affected. They are more susceptible to economic instability and gender-based violence as a result of this relocation. Climate change exacerbates the condition known as the "feminization of poverty," in which women are more likely than males to live in poverty.

Women's limited access to resources and decision-making processes makes it more difficult for them to adjust to changing environmental conditions, which feeds the cycles of marginalization and poverty. Implementing inclusive policies that enable women to take an active role in climate action and addressing the interwoven issues of marginalization and climate change require a sophisticated understanding of gender dynamics. Addressing the climate problem in a way that is equitable, sustainable, and successful requires an understanding of women's particular vulnerabilities and strengths.

Natural disasters like storms, floods, and landslides are examples of short-term negative effects of climate change, whereas more gradual environmental deterioration is an example of long-term bad effects. "Gender neutrality" is not applicable to the climate catastrophe. The effects of climate change are particularly felt by women and girls, exacerbating gender inequality. It jeopardizes the livelihoods, safety, security, health, and way of life of women and girls around the world. Roles, duties, decision-making, opportunities, requirements, and access to land and natural resources are all different for men and women. Women experience the most detrimental effects and are disproportionately impacted by climate change among the marginalized groups. Compared to men, women are more likely to live in poverty, have less access to democratic freedom and civil rights, and be victims of systemic violence, which often gets worse during turbulent times. The aim of this research was to find the association between the marginalization of women and the impact of climate change.

Statistics on the Effects of Climate Change and Women's Marginalization: Approximately 2.4 billion working-age women lack equal access to economic opportunities, and 178 nations still impose legislative restrictions that prevent them from fully participating in the economy.

Impact of Climate catastrophes: Due in large part to their restricted access to resources, information, mobility, and decision-making, women and children are 14 times more likely than males to perish during natural catastrophes.

Climate-Related Displacement: Women and girls are thought to make up 80% of those displaced by climate change.

Health hazards: Pregnancy difficulties and exposure to vector-borne infections, which are associated with poor outcomes for both mothers and newborns, are among the health hazards that climate change increases for women.

Health Risks: Women are more vulnerable to vector-borne infections and pregnancy difficulties due to climate change, which can have a negative impact on both the mother and the newborn.

REVIEW OF LITERATURE

Adenike and Obafemi (2020) in their research on the vulnerability of women to climate change in coastal regions of Nigeria discovered that women were vulnerable in all situations, regardless of the subtle ties of the values, patriarchal norms, environmental, economic, and socio-cultural factors that determine the roles of women and their interactions. This intersection of contextual factors goes beyond patriarchal traditions and is forged in the nexus between contextual investigation of climate change parameters and a localized investigation.

Farhana Sultana (2014), in her research on Gendering climate change demonstrates on how geographical insights may be used to better inform current policy narratives and adaptation programs. It finds the gendered implications of climate change in South Asia.

Cecilia Sorensen and Sujata Saunik (2018), from their research on Climate Change and Women's Health: found that the impact of climate change on health differs for men and women due to underlying socio-economic, cultural, and physiological factors. Although gender has been incorporated into international climate policy more and more, India has not made much progress in reducing gender-based health disparities or involving women in disaster risk reduction and management, climate change adaptation, and mitigation.

METHODOLOGY

The major goals of this research were to identify the specific vulnerabilities that women face as a result of climate change, as well as how these vulnerabilities are influenced by socio-economic status, location, and cultural norms, to find the direct and indirect effects of climate change on women's livelihood, health, and well-being and to study the factors that help or hinder women's ability to adapt to climate change and provide evidence-based recommendations for gender-sensitive policies and interventions that will empower them and promote sustainable development.

In this study descriptive research design was adopted. Through Convenience sampling thirty respondents who reside in and around Tirusulam, Chennai, were selected for the study. The research instrument for gathering data was a Questionnaire which had a structured list of statements intended to elicit information. Data collection included both primary and secondary sources.

FINDINGS

Seventy-seven percent (77%) of the respondents were within the age group of 26 – 35 years.

Fifty percent (50%) of the respondents were under graduates.

Eighty-three percent (83%) of the respondents were home makers.

Ninety-seven percent (97%) of the respondents were married and having school going children.

Seventy percent (70%) of the respondents said that their family experienced the direct impacts of climate change.

Ninety percent (90%) of the respondents agreed that climate change affects men and women differently.

Forty-seven percent (47%) of the respondents felt that they were marginalized in society.

Fifty percent (50%) of the respondents reported that they experienced many health-related issues like chicken pox, heavy fever, cold, etc. due to climate change.

Fifty percent (50%) of the respondents agreed that there was a relationship between climate change and marginalization of women.

Eighty-seven percent (87%)of the respondents reported rainy weather patterns, and 56.7% reported increased temperatures. 50% of respondents stated that lack of water availability.

Ninety-three percent (93%) of respondents reported that climate change has an impact on their health.

Ninety percent (90%) of respondents replied that climate change is affecting men and women differently.

Particulars	**5**	**4**	**3**	**2**	**1**	**Total ∑Wx**	**∑Wx/x**	**Rank**
How strongly do you agree or disagree 1.that climate change has affected your access to clean water?	10	92	6	2	2	112	7.466	VII

2.That you have experienced changes in food availability or quality due to climate change?	10	96	6	2	1	115	7.666	III
3.That climate change has affected your health or the health of your family?	5	96	6	2	2	111	7.4	VIII
4.That extreme weather events, such as floods or droughts, have impacted your community?	5	100	6	2	1	114	7.6	V
5.That you have noticed changes in the availability of natural resources, such as firewood or medicinal plants, due to climate change?	0	104	6	2	1	113	7.533	VI
6.That climate change has affected your ability to earn a living?	5	96	6	2	2	111	7.4	IX
7.That you have faced challenges in accessing education or other services due to climate change?	10	100	3	2	1	116	7.733	II
8.That you have had to relocate or consider relocating due to	5	68	9	16	1	99	6.6	X

climate change?								
9.That climate change has affected your cultural practices or traditions?	10	96	6	2	1	115	7.666	IV
10.That support is needed to help marginalized women adapt to the impacts of climate change?	0	112	3	2	0	117	7.8	I

Weighted Average Analysis- Impact of Climate Change

Impact of Climate Change

In this research the weighted average approach was used to identify and rank the different consequences of climate change that the respondents encountered. Despite the challenges they faced, the top three responses were: "support is needed to help marginalized women adapt to the impacts of climate change" (7.8%), "challenges in accessing education or other services due to climate change" (7.73%), and "relocation or considering relocation due to climate change" (6.6%). These findings underscore the critical need for targeted interventions to address the specific vulnerabilities of marginalized women in the face of climate change.

Hypothesis Statement	**Questions asked**	**Samples**	**Test used**	**T value**	**H_0** Null Hypothesis	**H_1** Alternate Hypothesis
H_0 – There is no relationship between the interaction of female, climate change and marginalization **H_1** – There is relationship between the interaction of female, climate change and marginalization	Rate your view, that there is a relationship between the interaction of female, climate change and marginalization	Set A – 13, 50, 30 Set B – 6, 1	Two tailed T - test	0.1428	**Rejected**	**Accepted** (T value > 0)

Two Tailed T-test

Two tailed Test

In this research the two tailed test was conducted to find the relationship between the factors climate change and marginalisation of women. The null hypothesis was rejected and the alternative hypothesis was accepted.

There is a relationship between climate change and marginalization of women.

SUGGESTIONS

1. Legal and Policy Reforms:

Eliminate Legal Barriers: Advocate for the removal of laws that restrict women's economic participation, ensuring equal rights in employment, property ownership, and access to financial services.

Implement Gender-Responsive Climate Policies: Develop and enforce policies that consider the unique challenges faced by women in the context of climate change, promoting their active participation in decision-making processes.

2. Economic Empowerment:

Access to Education and Training: Provide women with education and vocational training, particularly in sustainable practices and green technologies, to enhance their employment opportunities.

Support Female Entrepreneurship: Facilitate access to credit, markets, and networks for women entrepreneurs, enabling them to establish and grow businesses that contribute to climate resilience.

3. Health and Social Services:

Strengthen Healthcare Systems: Ensure that healthcare services are equipped to address climate-induced health issues, with a focus on maternal and reproductive health.

Provide Social Safety Nets: Establish support systems for women affected by climate-related displacement, including access to housing, education, and employment opportunities.

4. Community Engagement and Education:

Promote Women's Leadership: Encourage and support women's participation in community leadership roles, particularly in climate adaptation and disaster risk reduction initiatives.

Raise Awareness: Conduct community education programs to challenge gender norms that contribute to women's vulnerability during climate disasters.

CONCLUSION

Specific interventions are desperately needed to address these issues. It is important to include marginalized women in planning and implementation of Interventions. In all the steps starting from community needs assessments, capacity building, infrastructure development, healthcare access, and livelihood diversification the marginalised need to be involved. Building resilient communities that can endure the difficulties of a changing climate requires empowered women to actively engage in adaptation and mitigation measures.

REFERENCES

1. Adenike and Obafemi (2020) Vulnerability of women to Climate Change in coastal regions of Nigeria: A case of the Ilaje community in Ondo State. Journal of cleaner production. Volume 246.

2. Farhana Sultana (2014) Gendering climate change: Geographical insights. The Professional Geographer 66 (3), 372-381, 2014.

3. Cecilia Sorensen and Sujata Saunik (2018) Climate Change and Women's Health: Impacts and Opportunities in India. Geohealth. 2018 Oct; 2(10): 283–297. PMCID: PMC7007102.

4. Isabelle Anguelovski and James Connolly (2022) Intersectional Climate Justice: A conceptual pathway for bridging adaptation planning, transformative action, and social equity. Urban Climate 41, 101053.

17. A Study on Substance use and its Influence on Career Development of Youth in Perumbakkam, Chennai

Ms. Trisha Rebecca Leslie. A, II MSW & Mr. J. P. Francis Dhivakar, Assistant Professor, Department of Social Work, SFS, Madras Christian College

INTRODUCTION

Substance use refers to the misuse of legal substances and illegal substances that can be consumed, injected, inhaled or otherwise absorbed into the body. According to a definition given by the World Health Organization (WHO) Substance use refers to the harmful or hazardous use of psychoactive substances. The intake can lead to criminal or anti-social behaviour, long term changes in personality, harm to health, psychological problems and social problems.

This research aims to find the impact of substance use on the career development of the youth in Perumbakkam, a project area of the Urban Habitat and Development Board of Tamil Nadu.

REVIEW OF LITERATURE

Dan Lubman, Hides, Yucel and John Toumbourou (2007) in their study titled "Intervening early to reduce developmentally harmful substance use among youth population" highlight the adverse effects of substance use and the strategies and interventions that can prevent substance use. They strongly advocate that these interventions should be done at the early stage. Prevention programs are essential for children, adolescents and youth in families to have effective control on substance use. Dechenla and Ranabir (2009) in their study titled "Role of Family and Peers in Initiation and Continuation of Substance Use" have found that the causes for substance use are family and peer pressure.

Substance abuse starts at the early adolescence stage. The study states that early addiction leads to life time addiction. Family members and peers have a main role in influencing the youth to get into substance use. A descriptive cross-sectional study of Alexander, Jisha, Renjulal and

Nayak (2024) titled "Peer Influence and its Impact on Behaviour" conducted among the South Indian adolescents show that peer influence is a major cause for addiction.

METHODOLOGY

The aim of the study was to understand the factors contributing to substance use and its impact on the career development of youth in Perumbakkam. The general objective was to find the impact of substance use on career development of the youth in Perumbakkam. Descriptive research design and Convenience sampling methods were used in this study. The respondents were above 18 years old. Data was collected from thirty respondents. Interview Schedule was used for data collection.

FINDINGS

Sixty percent (60%) of the respondents were male.

Thirty-three percent (33%) of the respondents were between 23-27 years.

Forty percent (40%) of the respondents were married.

Ninety-three percent (93%) of them lived in a nuclear family.

Forty-seven percent (47%) were Hindu.

Ninety-four percent (94%) of respondents belonged to low-income group and their family income was less than Rs. 20,000/-

Thirty-three percent (33%) of the respondents were employed.

Ninety-three percent (93%) of the respondents were aware of the prevalence of substance use in their community.

Eighty-three percent (83%) reported that the youth engage in substance use regularly.

Seventy-three percent (73%) of the respondents consider peer pressure as the major factors contributing to substance use.

Fifty-three percent (53%) of the respondents agreed that media is a reason for substance use.

Sixty-three percent (63%) of the respondents stated that there should be strict rules and regulations to prevent sale of harmful substances in the community.

Sixty percent (60%) of the respondents reported that the career development opportunities are fair enough for youth's career growth and development.

Seventy-seven percent (77%) of the respondents have reported that pursuing and sustaining a career is a challenge.

Fifty-three percent (53%) of the respondents reported that they have not engaged in substance abuse whereas other 47% have reported that they have engaged in substance use.

Eighty-seven percent (87%) have observed the negative impact of substance use on their career development.

Forty percent (40%) of the respondents agreed that they have motivated persons addicted to substance use to quit.

Seventy-three percent (73%) of the respondents have not participated in any of the community programs addressing substance use and its negative impact.

Sixty-seven percent (67%) of the respondents agreed that there are support systems available in the area to mitigate the negative impact of substance use.

RECOMMENDATIONS

- To provide awareness and education on negative impact of substance abuse on personal life and career.

- To form support systems with the help of different NGOs in the community to give counselling and rehabilitation services and also mental health services for the youth affected by substance abuse.

- To provide skill development training and to create job opportunities.

• Strict enforcement machinery to prevent sale of harmful substances in the community.

CONCLUSION

In this study it was found that substance abuse had a negative impact on the career development of youth in Perumbakkam. The causes for substance abuse are peer pressure, media influence, socio-economic challenges and limited support systems. There is a significant need for strengthening the support networks, promoting awareness, advocating stricter regulations, providing skill in dealing with peer pressure and career development training and creating job opportunities. The Tamil Nadu Habitat Board need to collaborate with other stakeholders such as NGOs, youth associations and family members for a sustainable future of Youth in Perumbakkam.

REFERENCES

1. Dan Lubman, Hides, Yucel, John Toumbourou (2007) Intervening early to reduce developmentally harmful substance use among youth.

2. Dechencla and Ranabir (2009) Role of family and Peers in Initiation and Continuation of Substance Use.

3. Shohreh Akhavan, Sara Arti, Leila Qaraat, Geramian, Farajzadegan and Heidari (2014) A Review Study of Substance Abuse Status in High School.

4. Raphael, Raveendran, Sajna (2017) Prevalence and Determinants of Substance Abuse among youth in Central Kerala.

5. Konyukhova, Rodionova, Ekaterina, Osokina, Suhushina (2018) Specifics of interaction with youth prone to Substance Abuse.

6. Shraddha Balasaheb, Rohini Suryabhan, Tejas Uddhav (2022) A Review on Drug Abuse Among Youth.

7. Layman, Thorisdottir, Halldorsdottir Dora, John Allengrante and Logi Kristjansson (2022) Substance Use Among Youth During the Covid-19 Pandemic: A Systematic Review.

8. Alexander, Jisha, Renjulal, Nayak (2024) Peer influence and its impact on behaviour among South Indian Adolescents: A descriptive cross - sectional study.

18. The Legacy of Comfort Women and the Path Towards Reconciliation of Historical Injustice

Caroline Veronica. V

II PG, Department of International Studies, Loyola College, Chennai

Many fourteen-year-old children from South Korea, China and the Philippines were abducted, forced and tortured into sexual slavery under the soldiers who were serving the imperial government of Japan during the Second World War. Those children are now ninety-year-old women who are euphemistically called "Comfort Women." These women have not only been mistreated, but have also been disrespected, and forgotten. Immediate action is required for Japan to acknowledge and truly apologise for the pain and suffering of the victims by addressing the historical injustice that occurred.

The imperial Japanese army systemized sex trafficking and established camps that forced many young girls into sexual slavery. This was established to maintain "troop morale" among the Japanese imperial army. The camps began in Manchuria and eventually spread to over thirteen Southeast Asian colonies enslaving 200,000 victims from 1931 to 1945 until the end of the Second World War. These women were often "recruited" under false pretences, of jobs that paid during a financially rocky time for many families.

They were offered jobs like uniform stitching or being a first aid nurse. They were also kidnapped, purchased from parents or coerced into becoming comfort women. They were treated brutally, tortured inhumanely every one of them experiencing agonizing pain, pregnancies and sexually transmitted diseases that were often not treated properly. They had to "serve" the Japanese armed forces from twelve to six pm on the weekdays and from 8 am to 5 pm at the end of the week. Each girl had to fill a quota of forty men a day in a queue.

The comfort camps were often referred to as "Public toilets." The young girls even considered suicide because of self-shame but were unsuccessful in their attempts. Some of them purposefully lived on to talk about it. More than ninety percent of the comfort women passed away amid the war and a few of the survivors died of untreated complications from STDs.

Kim Hak Sun was one of the brave survivors who broke the silence on August 14th 1991. She was abducted at the age of seventeen. Two hundred and eight women stepped forward following her confession. One of them was Kim Bik Dong. Kim Bok Dong was recruited under false pretenses for a uniform stitching job at the age of fourteen. She was the youngest among a group of thirty-two women who were between fourteen to twenty years of age.

In an interview with Asian Boss, when asked what they are fighting for, Kim Bok Dong said: "What I want is an apology from the Japanese Government for dragging us away and making us suffer. I want a formal apology. They should say "What we did was completely wrong and we'll correct our history textbooks. And say to us "We sincerely apologise. If they wrote that kind of formal apology, then we can forgive them. This is not about the money. They keep trying to make this issue go away. And we're the ones who are constantly fighting so that it doesn't happen. It's History!" (Kim, 2018)

The Korean Council for Women was Drafted for Military Sexual Slavery by Japan and the Korean Government created the Comfort Women statue to represent the pain and plight of these women. The statue is of a young girl in a traditional Hanbok worn by many during the abduction. They are barefoot with their heel lifted to represent unrest. Her hands are clenched and her face is dignified. The statue's base has a mosaic of older women to represent the comfort women who are now growing older. There is a tiny bird on the shoulder of the girl to represent the fight for freedom.

The empty chair next to the girl represents the many women who are no more and is also an invitation to the visitors to reflect on the past and fight with the women for freedom. During monsoon and winter times, many people leave umbrellas and scarves on the statue. Many also leave flowers during the spring season. The Japanese government has repeatedly refused to acknowledge Japan's past actions. Former Prime Minister of Japan, Shinzo Abe claimed that Japan's reputation is being tarnished under the fact that there is no physical evidence of the abuse.

In July 2020, Kim Chang Ryul the president of the Korean Botanical Garden erected the statue of a man apologising to a comfort woman. The Japanese Government claims that there is a resemblance to Prime Minister Shinzo Abe. The issue continues to exasperate with no resolution in sight. Many survivors are now no more and only youth and volunteers are fighting for these women. Mr Kim says that the statue represents a person in any position who was at fault or anyone who could be in a position to apologise.

Kim Bok Dong says that she regrets coming forward because she didn't expect this issue to drag out for so long. When asked if she would forgive the soldiers for their behaviour. She said "Hate the Sin, not the Sinner" and that she will forgive them. In an interview with Asian Boss she says, "At the age of 14, when I should've been studying, I was taken away. Not being able to study is my deepest regret. At this age, when I should be at peace, the Japanese Government keeps dragging out this issue." She also says, "So, whenever I have to talk about this over and over, I'm heartbroken beyond belief."

Ms Kim Bok Dong passed away at ninety-three, not having forgiven the Japanese Government. She passed away not having received any compensation for her sufferings which she only wanted to donate to other girls who could not afford to study. Many more women passed away not having resolved their sufferings.

True inclusivity goes beyond merely accepting each other. It involves actively reconciling historical injustice and acknowledging past mistakes. Inclusivity is only when we recognise each other for our true selves, our diverse backgrounds, experiences and perspectives. It is about building an environment where everyone feels seen, heard, and valued, and where the scars of history are addressed with honesty and compassion. Inclusivity is an ongoing commitment to equity, understanding, and mutual respect, ensuring all individuals are empowered to thrive and contribute to a more just and harmonious society.

REFERENCES

1. Asian Boss. (2018). Life As A "Comfort Woman": Story of Kim Bok-Dong | Stay Curious #9. Youtube. https://www.youtube.com/watch?v=qsT97ax_Xb0 2. Blakemore, Erin. (2023, May 31). Comfort women: Japan's military brothels. History. https://www.history.com/news/comfort-women-japan-military-brothels-korea 3. Dudden, Alexis. (2022, September 16). Guide to Understanding the History of the Comfort Women Issue. U.S Institute of Peace.

2. https://www.usip.org/publications/2022/09/guide-understanding-history-comfort-wom en-issue

3. Gilbert, L. D. (2021). The Deterioration of U.S.-ROK-Japan Trilateral Security Cooperation: Diverging Threat Perceptions and Conflicting National Strategic Identities. https://s-space.snu.ac.kr/bitstream/10371/179051/1/000000168040.pdf

4. Hosaka, Yuji. (2021, November 11). Why did the 2015 Japan-Korea 'Comfort Women' Agreement Fall Apart? The Diplomat.

5.https://thediplomat.com/2021/11/why-did-the-2015-japan-korea-comfort-women-agre ement-fall-apart/

6. Hu, Elise. (2017, November 13). Comfort Women memorial status, a thorn in Japan's side, now sit on Korean buses. NPR.

7.https://www.npr.org/sections/parallels/2017/11/13/563838610/comfort-woman-memorial-statues-a-thorn-in-japans-side-now-sit-on-korean-buses

8. Kerry, John. (2015, December 17). Remarks at the 2015 International Conference on the Comfort Women Issue. U.S. Department of State.

9. https://2009-2017.state.gov/secretary/remarks/2015/12/250874.htm

10. Kwon, Y., & Park, H. Y. (2023). New ways of solidarity with Korean comfort women: Comfort women and what remains. Palgrave Macmillan.

11.https://dokumen.pub/new-ways-of-solidarity-with-korean-comfort-women-comfort-w omen-and-what-remains-palgrave-macmillan-studies-on-human-rights-in-asia-1st-edition2023-981991793x 9789819917938.html

12.Ministry of Foreign Affairs of Japan. (2020, July). Postwar diplomacy.
https://www.mofa.go.jp/policy/postwar/page22e_000883.html

13. Rosenburg, J. (2023, October 21). Overlooked No More: Kim Hak Soon, who broke the silence for comfort women. The New York Times.

14.https://www.nytimes.com/2021/10/21/obituaries/kim-hak-soon-overlooked.html 11. Uncharted History. (2024, June). Gut-Wrenching Things That Happened to Comfort Women. Youtube. https://www.youtube.com/watch?v=5OBxinJMGIw 12. Wadhwa, Mrinalini. (2021, March 17). Resolution for WWII comfort women: Korea, Japan, and the International Court of Justice. ColumbiaUndergraduateLawReview.https://www.culawreview.org/journal/resolution-for-wwii-comfort-women-korea-japa n-and-the-international-court-of-justice

15. Wasson, K. R. (2018). Discomforting Neighbors: Emotional Communities Clash over "Comfort Women" in an American Town (Doctoral dissertation, University of California, Santa Barbara). https://escholarship.org/

19. A Study on Awareness and Perception of HIV/AIDS among College Students

Ms. A. Arockya Vianny Sweatha, II MSW HRM &
Mr. J.P Francis Dhivakar, Assistant Professor,
Department of Social Work, SFS, Madras Christian College

INTRODUCTION

The awareness of HIV/AIDS among youth is vital for effective prevention and intervention strategies. Understanding youth perceptions of HIV/AIDS is vital for removal of social stigma. Despite advancements in medical treatment and public health campaigns, youth remain vulnerableto HIV/AIDS due to socio-cultural factors. Globally, HIV/AIDS continues to pose a significant health challenge, affecting millions, particularly the youth. This study aims to explore the awareness and perception of HIV/AIDS among college students to prevent societal stigma.

The general objective of the study was to explore and gain insights into the perception and awareness of HIV/AIDS among college students in Tambaram. The specific objectives were to assess the knowledge and awareness of HIV/AIDS among the respondents, to find the misconceptions prevalent among the respondents about HIV/AIDS and to give suggestions to for effective prevention of HIV/AIDS and remove social stigma attached to HIV/AIDS.

REVIEW OF LITERATURE

In 2017, Subbarao and Akhilesh conducted a study among 350 engineering college students. They studied the knowledge and attitude of the college students towards STIs (excluding HIV). While 90% had heard of STIs, only 64% were aware of non-HIV STIs, and less than 50% knew their symptoms and complications. The main sources of information were teachers, internet, and media. Despite 75% being aware of transmission modes, knowledge of prevention and treatment was limited, and attitudes toward sexual health varied. The study underscores the need for better sexual health education to prevent STIs and related complications.

In 2015, Choudhary, Ali and Altaf conducted a cross-sectional study to assess the knowledge, behavior and attitudes of 469 undergraduate students at an Irish university regarding HIV/AIDS. The study found that over 95% of participants identified primary HIV/AIDS transmission routes, with males more aware of personal risk than females (p=0.03). Despite this, 82.5% had never tested for HIV, 43% engaged in unprotected sex, and 42% felt a need for HIV/AIDS prevention education. The findings highlight a gap between knowledge and behaviour, emphasizing the need for enhanced education and strategies to promote awareness, prevention and safer sexual practices.

METHODOLOGY & MAJOR FINDINGS

In this study Descriptive research design was adopted. Convenience Sampling method was used to collect data from the respondents. The IV-KQ-18 tool was used to collect data from the respondents.

The demographic details of the participants reveal a predominantly female representation, with 70% females and 30% males. Most participants 53.3% were between 20-30 years followed by 43.3% in the age group of 18-20 years and a small proportion 3.4% in the age group of 30 years and above. Most of the respondents 96.7% were unmarried.

In terms of educational background, participants were almost evenly split, with 53.3% of undergraduates and 46.7% postgraduates. Urban residents formed the majority 74% whereas rural participants accounted for 26%. Additionally, 60% of the respondents were from other districts with 40% being natives of Chennai. Notably, 80% of the participants did not have a science background.

A significant number of respondents 66.7% correctly understood that sneezing & coughing doesn't spread HIV and 73.3% rightly understood that sharing a glass of water does not transmit HIV. Misconceptions were evident in several areas. For instance, only 46.7% correctly identified that pulling out the penis before ejaculation does not prevent HIV transmission during sex, with 36.7% incorrectly believing it does. While 63.3% recognized that HIV can be transmitted through anal sex and a similar percentage 63.3% disagreed that showering after sex prevents HIV hence it is interpreted that there were notable gaps in knowledge. For example, only 43.3% understood that not all HIV-infected mothers give birth to HIV-positive babies, highlighting a lack of awareness about mother-to-child transmission.

The respondents' understanding about HIV symptoms and testing timelines was limited, with 70% rightly recognizing that infected individuals may not quickly show serious symptoms and only 43.3% knowing that testing immediately after sex does not confirm HIV status. Furthermore, 53.3% knew there is no vaccine to prevent HIV, yet misconceptions persisted about HIV transmission through deep kissing and many were unclear about the effectiveness of natural skin condoms, with only 53.3% rightly disagreeing that they work better than latex condoms.

Encouragingly, 80% were aware that having multiple sexual partners increased the risk of HIV infection and 76.7% correctly identified that using Vaseline or baby oil with condoms do not lower the risk of getting HIV. However, there was confusion regarding oral sex, with only 56.7% acknowledging it as a potential route for HIV transmission. Overall, while participants demonstrated a fair understanding of basic HIV transmission and prevention, there were critical knowledge gaps and persistent misconceptions. The results emphasize the importance of targeted educational interventions to bridge these gaps & prevent social stigma.

The study reveals that students with a science background and PG level education scored higher in HIV/AIDS knowledge. Most respondents demonstrated good awareness of HIV transmission. While basic knowledge is high, critical misconceptions about transmission, prevention & testing highlight the need for targeted education efforts to improve understanding and reduce knowledge gaps.

SUGGESTIONS & CONCLUSION

HIV/AIDS prevention education to be started from school.

To improve HIV/AIDS awareness among college students by promoting community engagement programs.

To create awareness on HIV/AIDS through Digital Media Campaigns.

To organise stigma reduction programs involving key stakeholders at all levels for Social Inclusion of the HIV infected persons.

This study highlights the importance of understanding youth perceptions of HIV/AIDS to create effective prevention strategies. It aims to reduce stigma, improve risk perception and enhance public health outcomes. Over half of the respondents demonstrated awareness. The study recommends community engagement programs and inclusion of HIV/AIDS related content in the higher education curriculum for the students to gain knowledge about the same and improve Social Inclusion of the HIV infected persons.

REFERENCES

1. Al Rabeei, N. A., Dallak, A. M., & Al Awadi, F. G. (2012). Knowledge, attitude and beliefs towards HIV. EMHJ-Eastern Mediterranean Health Journal, 18 (3), 221-226, 2012.

2. Choudhary, H. A., Ali, R. A., & Altaf, S. (2015). Knowledge, behaviour and attitudes regarding HIV/AIDS among undergraduate students in an Irish university. International Journal of Surgery and Medicine, 1(2), 58-66.

3. Murray, A., Huang, M. J., Hardnett, F., & Sutton, M. Y. (2014). Strengthening HIV knowledge and awareness among undergraduate students at historically black colleges and universities. Journal of Health Disparities Research and Practice, 7(4).

www.ingramcontent.com/pod-product-compliance
Lightning Source LLC
LaVergne TN
LVHW021139160826
845679LV00023B/1972

9798897440658